Academic English

Academic English
Skills for Success

Second Edition

Miranda Legg
Kevin Pat
Steve Roberts
Rebecca Welland
Letty Chan
Louisa Chan
Wai Lan Tsang

香港大學出版社
HONG KONG UNIVERSITY PRESS

Hong Kong University Press
The University of Hong Kong
Pokfulam Road
Hong Kong
www.hkupress.org

ISBN 978-988-8208-64-7

British Library Cataloguing-in-Publication Data
A catalogue record for this book is available from the British Library.

10 9 8 7 6 5 4 3 2 1

Printed and bound by Paramount Printing Co., Ltd. in Hong Kong, China

Contents

UNIT 1 HEALTH   1
Introduction to features of academic writing and speaking

UNIT 2 GLOBAL ISSUES   31
Note-taking and paraphrasing

UNIT 3 ETHICS
61

Expressing stance

ACADEMIC SPEAKING

UNIT 4 CHINA AND ASIA
Synthesizing ideas in a paragraph or section

ACADEMIC WRITING

ACADEMIC SPEAKING

UNIT 5 VALUES
Structuring a complete academic text

ACADEMIC WRITING

Textbook map

Unit	Topic		Focus on Writing	Focus on Speaking
1	HEALTH	Introduction to features of academic writing and speaking	• recognize the basic features of academic writing at university level • search for and evaluate academic sources of information • identify different types of supporting evidence	• integrate different types of academic sources • recognize the purpose and features of a tutorial discussion
2	GLOBAL ISSUES	Note-taking and paraphrasing	• analyze assignment topics • synthesize and link ideas through note-taking and paraphrasing • reference multiple sources concurrently to strengthen evidence relating to your stance	• identify the similarities/ differences between written and spoken texts • transform written language into spoken language during a tutorial discussion
3	ETHICS	Expressing stance	• identify features of a successful academic stance • write a stance which has an academic tone, is reasonable and well-justified • integrate counter-arguments and rebuttals into a stance to make it more critical	• express agreement and disagreement with the stance of others in speaking • use questions to make a tutorial discussion more critical and thoughtful
4	CHINA and ASIA	Synthesizing ideas in a paragraph/ section	• logically connect ideas within a paragraph or a section • write accurate and appropriate section headings • connect ideas through the use of cohesive devices and strategies	• link your speaking turn to what has been previously said • change focus within an academic discussion
5	VALUES	Structuring a complete academic text	• apply a range of structural features to help you organize an academic text • recognize the similarities and differences in report and essay structures • create connections across paragraphs and sections	• reflect on your discussion skills • articulate strategies to improve your discussion skills in the future

Acknowledgements

A large number of people have contributed to the development of this textbook. The authors specifically wish to thank the following:

- The authors of the first edition: Letty Chan, Louisa Chan and Wai Lan Tsang.

- The University of Hong Kong for the Teaching Development Grant, which funded the writing of the first edition of this textbook.

- All of the teaching staff of the Centre for Applied English Studies at the University of Hong Kong who have taught this course and given feedback on the materials.

- The students who have also generously given feedback on the materials.

- Professor Ken Hyland, Dr Agnes Lam, Dr David Gardner and Eliza Yu who have given guidance along the way.

Introduction for students

Aims

This textbook aims to:

- help you make the transition from studying at a secondary school to studying at an English-medium university,

- develop the general academic English skills you will need to complete your undergraduate degree at university.

Learning outcomes

By the end of the textbook you should be able to:

- identify features of academic writing and speaking,
- search for and evaluate academic sources,
- take effective notes and paraphrase from sources,
- express a personal and critical stance,
- synthesize ideas within a paragraph/section, and
- structure a complete academic text.

How to make the most of this textbook

Apply skills practised in this textbook to your other courses.

The work you do in this textbook should be useful in many, if not all, of your university courses. You should make a concerted effort to apply what you learn in this textbook to the writing and speaking you do in other courses.

Participate actively.

By the end of this textbook you will have practised your academic writing, read a number of academic texts, and participated in a series of academic speaking tutorials. Many of these tasks will require you to interact with your classmates in order to benefit from a variety of perspectives. You will get the most out of these tasks if you participate actively in and out of class.

Do complementary work.

Your teacher may supplement the work in this textbook with other work on grammar, vocabulary, citation and referencing skills and tasks on how to avoid plagiarism. This work is very important and will help you to achieve the aims listed above.

1
HEALTH

Introduction to features of academic writing and speaking

Learning outcomes

By the end of this unit, you should be able to:

- ▸ recognize the basic features of academic writing at university level,
- ▸ search for and evaluate academic sources of information,
- ▸ evaluate the quality of these sources,
- ▸ identify different types of supporting evidence, and
- ▸ recognize the purpose and features of a tutorial discussion.

ACADEMIC WRITING

Task 1
Reflect on the health care system in your country

In 1946, the World Health Organization (WHO) defined health as "a state of complete physical, mental, and social well-being and not merely the absence of disease or infirmity". Health care systems within countries therefore aim to organize people, institutions and resources in order to promote the broad definition of health offered by the WHO.

Use the table below to circle the type of health care system used in your country and rate your opinion of this system's impact on society's physical, mental and social well-being.

Circle the structure of health care in your country	Your opinion of this system's impact on . . .	
direct payment by the user	**. . . physical well-being** (e.g. its influence on physical disease)	poor ⸻ excellent
taxes from the public	**. . . mental well-being** (e.g. its influence on mental illnesses)	poor ⸻ excellent
national health insurance	**. . . social well-being** (e.g. its ability to cater for the health needs of **all** groups of people within a society)	poor ⸻ excellent
private health insurance		
a combination of the above		

Now share your thoughts with a partner and try to reach a consensus regarding the strengths and weaknesses of the health care system in your country.

Task 2

Discuss the success of the health care system

Your teacher will put you in groups of four and assign each member a different health issue as follows:

A: Obesity
B: Smoking
C: Stress
D: Air pollution

Imagine you are part of a government committee deciding how to reform the health care system in your country. However, there are only enough funds to reform one health issue. Your aim is to gain these funds to tackle the issue assigned to you by:

1. explaining the possible shortcomings of the current system in dealing with your assigned issue, and

2. suggesting practical solutions to this problem.

Use the table below to prepare your argument.

Improving our health care system
Your assigned health issue
Reason(s) for my viewpoint
A practical solution

Task 3
Present and rate your ideas

Spend around ten minutes explaining your ideas to the rest of your group. When you are finished, use the criteria below to decide whose solution will be chosen by your committee.

	Obesity	Smoking	Stress	Air pollution
The ideas were easy to understand	Y/N	Y/N	Y/N	Y/N
Relevant reasons were given	Y/N	Y/N	Y/N	Y/N
The solution was practical	Y/N	Y/N	Y/N	Y/N

Task 4
Explore an argument in a written text

You are about to read either an essay (Group A) or a report (Group B) on a health-related topic. As you read, use the relevant space in the box below to:

1. note down the main arguments the writer makes, and

2. record the paragraph/section numbers which helped you identify these arguments.

Group A: Essay	
Argument	Paragraph number

Group B: Report	
Argument	Section number

Argument	Paragraph number	Argument	Section number

Now compare your answers with a student who read the same text as you. Then check your ideas on pages 140 and 141.

Essay Topic:

Who should pay for healthcare?

The issue of who should pay for healthcare is highly controversial and complex. <u>**Opinions on this issue are likely to be related to one's political views, ethical views, and socioeconomic status.**</u> Funding for healthcare tends to come from four major sources: direct payment by the user, taxes from the public, national health insurance and private health insurance. Upon closer investigation, these four sources can be further categorized into <u>**a government-provided healthcare system**</u> (taxation and national health insurance) and <u>**a user-paid system**</u> (private health insurance and direct payment by the user at the time of treatment). This essay will first discuss these two models of healthcare and afterwards <u>**argue that a combination of the two models is worth exploration and can serve as a blueprint for designing a more efficient healthcare system.**</u>

People from wealthy backgrounds tend to support <u>**a user-paid system**</u> based on the belief that this type of system provides more choice and better quality than a government-run system. However, an examination of the overall US healthcare model illustrates that this is often not true. Davis et al. (2007) report that <u>**"despite having the most costly health system in the world, the United States consistently underperforms on most dimensions of performance, relative to other countries"**</u> (p. 34). The ability to pay for a higher cost healthcare system does not necessarily translate to better quality. <u>**Another major argument**</u> for a user-paid system is that it is an individual's responsibility to pay if the individual has the funds to do so. Otherwise, government revenue would be required, which is also needed for a number of other critical public programmes such as education and new infrastructure. Therefore, in order to better maintain other government-funded programmes, those who are able should take individual responsibility for their healthcare. While this point is valid, <u>**the question of how those with insufficient economic means will be able to get healthcare remains unanswered.**</u>

A controversial solution to <u>**this question**</u> lies within <u>**a government-provided healthcare system**</u>. One clear benefit to government funding is that those who cannot afford healthcare are provided with it. If a large percentage of any population cannot afford medical care, productivity among that population would likely decrease in cases of illness. There is also research to suggest that people who have constant access to healthcare generally live healthier lives and cost the medical system less overall than those who go to

Stance

Organization

Stance

Organization

Citation

Organization

Organization

Organization

the doctor only in an emergency **(Williams 2005; Emerson 2006)**. The — Citation
higher upfront costs that the government would accrue initially could be
offset or eventually reduced by a decrease in the frequency of expensive
emergency visits. An illustrative example of this was highlighted by
Gawande (2011), who describes a preventative programme in the US that
resulted in net savings in healthcare costs that were "undoubtedly lower"
(para. 39). **However, arguments against a government-paid system still** — Stance
persist. According to Smith (2001), it is often politically unpopular, as
governments need to increase taxation as the population ages. This would
decrease the likelihood of success for governments to convince people that
a largely government-run system would be cheaper and more efficient. Few
politicians would want to damage their own political careers by instituting
higher taxation. **Thus, while shifting to a government-provided** — Organization
healthcare system would increase coverage for those who cannot afford
healthcare, new controversy and complexity would also be introduced.

In light of the benefits and deficiencies mentioned above, advocacy — Stance
for a combined approach to funding healthcare is crucial. In fact,
successful examples of a merger between the two healthcare systems are
already existent. Hong Kong operates both a government- and user-paid
healthcare system, broadening coverage for the entire community while
maintaining more personalized services and choices for those who are
able to afford them ("HK healthcare is a dual-track system", 2013). **The**
same article also notes impressive and comparable measures of health — Citation
in Hong Kong, with an infant mortality rate below 2 deaths per 1000
live births and an 80-year life expectancy. In a similar comparison,
Singapore employs a combined healthcare system. This combination has
allowed Singapore to ensure health coverage for the poor, prevent financial
destitution from catastrophic illness, and still preserve choices for those
more financially able (Lim, 2004). **Health outcomes indicate efficacy: a**
78.4 years in life expectancy, 2.2 per 1000 infant mortality rate, and
an 80% satisfaction rate for corporatized public hospitals (Lim, 2004).
However, it should be noted that Hong Kong and Singapore have unique
social and economic situations, and a population that, in contrast with
other developed nations, is significantly smaller and more manageable.
Nonetheless, they can be used as starting points for how a combined
approach to healthcare can be administered as supported by Haseltine
(2013), a noted Harvard professor and AIDS researcher, who believes
that an investigation of the Singaporean healthcare system should be a
requisite when government officials debate issues concerning healthcare
systems. This combined approach also helps to partially alleviate political
concerns about taxes mentioned previously as KPMG International (2012)

reports that Hong Kong and Singapore are among the lowest, globally, in personal income tax rates and have remained flat since 2004. Evidence from these countries is highly suggestive that a government-paid system in conjunction with a public-user-paid system, if implemented correctly and accordingly, can maintain the benefits and allay deficiencies in each of the systems operating individually.

What is clear is that deciding which party is responsible for funding healthcare costs is highly contentious. In response, this essay has discussed the benefits and deficiencies of a government-paid healthcare system and a public-user-paid system. Despite the possibility of higher taxes and inadequate allocation to other government-funded programmes, a government-paid healthcare system offers coverage to a wider number of people. However, proponents of a public-user-paid system believe that healthcare should be the responsibility of each individual. **In view of these arguments, a way forward is to establish a feasible combined healthcare system approach.** Using Singapore and Hong Kong as case studies, other nations should investigate how this approach can be successfully applied to their local contexts in order to minimize weaknesses in each individual healthcare system while maximizing their benefits.

Stance

References

Davis, C., C. Schoen, M. Schoenbaum, A. Doty, J. Holmgren, & K. Shea (2007). An international update on the comparative performance of American health care. *The Journal of International Health Education* 1(12): 125–204.

Emerson, A. (2006). Emergency care and its costs. *The Journal of Emergency Health* 2(24): 116–132.

Gawande, A. (2011, 24 January). The Hot Spotters: Can we lower medical costs by giving the neediest patients better care? *The New Yorker*. Retrieved from http://www.newyorker.com/reporting/2011/01/24/110124fa_fact_gawande?currentPage=all

Haseltine, W. A. (2013). *Affordable Excellence: The Singapore Healthcare Story*. Washington, D.C.: Brookings Institution Press.

Ko, W. M. (2013, 9 April). HK healthcare is a dual-track system. news.gov.hk. Retrieved from http://www.news.gov.hk/en/record/html/2013/04/20130409_190409.lin.shtml

KPMG International. (2012). *KPMG's Individual Income Tax and Social Security Rate Survey 2012*. Retrieved from http://www.kpmg.com/global/en/issuesandinsights/articlespublications/documents/individual-income-tax-rate-survey-2012.pdf

Lim, M. K. (2004). Shifting the burden of health care finance: A case study of public–private partnership in Singapore. *Health Policy* 69(1): 83–92.

Smith, J. (2001). Politics and the tax system. *The Journal of Tax, Economics, and Politics* 3(21): 280–300.

Williams, A. (2005). Benefits of preventative care. *The Journal of Preventative Care and Medicine* 2(26): 200–220.

Report Topic:

How serious is the problem of childhood obesity in developing countries?
What are the causes? What are some possible interventions to lower obesity rates?

1. Introduction

The obesity epidemic has been "spreading" from developed to developing countries (DCs). As countries rise out of poverty, their populations tend to develop a set of health conditions linked to their more affluent, urbanized lifestyle. This phenomenon is not only being seen in adults, but increasingly in children too. **This report will outline the seriousness of** ◄——— Organization **the childhood obesity problem in Asian DCs. It will then discuss the main causes of this problem** and **suggest a multifaceted approach to** ◄——— Stance **tackle this worrying public health problem.**

2. Seriousness of Childhood Obesity

    2.1 Growing Levels of Childhood Obesity

    Since there is currently no worldwide consensus regarding the definition of childhood obesity, it is very difficult to compare rates across countries. Different studies use different measures; some do not distinguish between being obese and overweight and some do. However, **a common definition of childhood obesity is a BMI** ◄——— Stance **greater than the 95th percentile, while the definition of being overweight is greater than the 85th percentile for children** [1].

    Despite differing measurements of obesity, some comparative research has been done to uncover trends in obesity in DCs. For example, one analysis of 160 nationally representative surveys from 94 DCs shows that obesity rates are increasing [2]. This phenomenon is mostly centred in urban areas of these countries [3] and the rates are much higher in older children (6–18) than in pre-schoolers [3].

    A different study focusing on China estimated that 12.9% of ◄——— Citation **children were overweight and of those, 6.5% were obese [4]. However, urban areas usually have much higher rates than this. In Dalian, for example, the overweight rates (including rates of obesity) were found to be 22.9% for boys and 10.4% for girls [5].**

    The rates for one urban area in India (Amritsar in the Punjab region) were slightly lower than in urban China: 14% of boys and 18.3% of girls aged 10–15 years were found to be overweight, and of those, 5% of boys and 6.3% of girls were obese [6]. The rate in Pakistan was similar: the overall rate of overweight and obesity in children was 5.7%. The rate in boys was 4.6% versus 6.4% in girls and these rates increased with age, rising to 7% and 11% for boys and girls aged 13–14 years [7].

These rates are not much different than those in the USA about 10 years ago. In 1998 the rates for 6 to 17-year-olds were 11% obese and 14% overweight [8]. Current rates are significantly higher, with 31.7% of the same age group overweight and 16.9% obese (2–19 years) [9]. This is an indicator of where many people in DCs might end up as they become more wealthy.

2.2 Consequences of Childhood Obesity
Severely overweight children are at risk of **developing skeletal [10], brain [11], lung [12] and hormonal [13] conditions.** Non-medical consequences are also severe. These include long-term effects on self-esteem, body image and also increased feelings of sadness and loneliness [14], largely as a result of peer rejection [15]. In severe cases, this rejection has been reported to lead to suicide [16]. The research into these long-term effects is scarce because high levels of childhood obesity are a relatively new phenomenon.

3. Major Causes of Childhood Obesity
Malnutrition used to be the focus of public health initiatives in DCs. Now, while malnutrition is still a problem in these contexts, so too is obesity. This is largely caused by rapid urbanization [3] and increased wealth. This link between economic progress and negative health consequences, sometimes called "New World Syndrome" [3], is extremely complicated. **However, there are mainly two factors at play: individuals' increasing energy consumption and decreasing energy expenditure through a lack of exercise.**

3.1 Increased energy consumption
The diet of people living in urban areas in DCs is vastly different from those living in rural areas [17] and includes consumption of a higher proportion of fat, sugar, animal products, and less fibre, often found in restaurant foods [17]. This diet leads to a higher consumption of energy than more "traditional" diets.

3.2 Reduced energy expenditure
This increase in energy consumption is at odds with a decrease in

Citation

Organization

Stance

energy consumption. As a country moves from an agricultural economy to an industrialized one, the energy expenditure of the population tends to decrease [18]. There has been a lot of research about the effect of this trend on adult energy expenditure. Once industrial processes become more computerized, employment moves to the service sector and a larger proportion of the population spend the working day behind a desk, leading to lower levels of activity and ultimately higher rates of obesity. Less is known about children. However, **as noted in Section 2.2**, insufficient research has been conducted on childhood obesity, and thus the changes in DC youths' energy expenditure and the consequent impact on childhood obesity remains unclear.

Organization

4. Suggested Interventions

Unfortunately, there is little chance of DCs averting an obesity pandemic in the future [19]. There is no reason to believe that they will be any more successful than developed countries, which have been **largely unsuccessful** in reducing rates of childhood obesity. Furthermore, DCs tend to have limited resources for large-scale intervention programmes through the public health sector and much of these populations associate a more "Westernized" lifestyle with an increase in social status and are therefore reluctant to give up, for example, eating in restaurants, watching a lot of TV, playing computer games, and travelling predominantly by car.

Stance

However, this does not mean that action should not be taken. **Although many of the underlying causes of obesity stem from much needed growth, for example, access to higher-paid employment in the service sector and increased economic wealth, interventions are needed, even if they have a limited effect in the near future.** Kruger et al. [20] suggest a model for South Africa that can serve as a useful starting point for DCs. They argue that obesity prevention and treatment should be based on:

Stance

+ education
+ behaviour change
+ political support
+ adequately resourced programmes
+ evidence-based planning
+ proper monitoring and evaluation

They also argue that interventions should have the following components:
+ reasonable weight goals
+ healthful eating
+ physical activity
+ behavioural change

This model might sound vague, but this is necessary as the specifics of what programme to run or what kind of political change is needed will depend heavily on the target country and even target region within that country as each country and region has its own unique set of conditions which require different adaptations of these interventions.

Stance

5. Conclusion

Obesity has become a pandemic and the incidence of childhood obesity is rising in DCs. Its causes are complicated but they predominantly relate to the changing social and economic conditions which develop as countries gain wealth, urbanize and industrialize. In order to tackle this worrying trend, interventions which target local needs are needed. **Even though medium-term success in lowering obesity rates is likely to be limited,** meeting modest targets such as a reduction in 1–2% of childhood obesity can have a future impact on the health outcomes of millions of inhabitants of DCs.

Stance

Stance

References

1. Must, A., & R. S. Strauss (1999). Risks and consequences of childhood and adolescent obesity. *International Journal of Obesity and Related Metabolic Disorders: Journal of the International Association for the Study of Obesity* 23 Suppl. 2: S2–11.

2. Onis, M., & M. Blossner (2000). Prevalence and trends of overweight among preschool children in developing countries. *American Journal of Clinical Nutrition* 72: 1032–1039.

3. Kelishadi, R. (2007). Childhood overweight, obesity, and the metabolic syndrome in developing countries. *Epidemiologic Reviews* 29: 62–76.

4. Wang, Y. (2001). Cross-national comparison of childhood obesity: The epidemic and the relationship between obesity and socio-economic status. *International Journal of Epidemiology* 30: 1129–1136.

5. Zhou, H., T. Yamauchi, & K. Natsuhara et al. (2006). Overweight in urban schoolchildren assessed by body mass index and body fat mass in Dalian, China. *Journal of Physiology and Anthropology* 25: 41–48.

6. Sidhu, S., G. Marwah, & Prabhjot. (2005). Prevalence of overweight and obesity among the affluent adolescent schoolchildren of Amritsar, Punjab. *Coll Antropol.* 29: 53–55.

7. Jafar, T. H., H. Qadri, M. Islam, J. Hatcher, Z. A. Bhutta, & N. Chaturvedi (2008). Rise in childhood obesity with persistently high rates of undernutrition among urban school-aged Indo-Asian children. *Arch Dis Child* 93: 373–378.

8. Troiano, R. P., & K. M. Flegal (1998). Overweight children and adolescents: Description, epidemiology, and demographics. *Pediatrics* 101(3): 497–504.

9. Ogden, C. L., M. D. Carroll, L. R. Curtin, M. M. Lamb, & K. M. Flegal (2010). Prevalence of high body mass index in US children and adolescents. *Journal of American Medical Association* 303(3): 242–249.

10. Dietz, W. H., W. L. Gross, & J. A. Kirkpatrick (1982). Blount disease (tibia vara): Another skeletal disorder associated with childhood obesity. *Journal of Pediatrics* 101: 735–737.

11. Scott, I. U., R. M. Siatkowski, M. Eneyni, M. C. Brodsky, & B. L. Lam (1997). Idiopathic intracranial hypertension in children and adolescents. *Am J Opth.* 124: 253–255.

12. Marcus, C. L., S. Curtis, C. B. Koerner, A. Joffe, J. R. Serwint, & G. M. Loughlin (1996). Evaluation of pulmonary function and polysomnography in obese children and adolescents. *Pediatr Pulmonol.* 21: 176–183.

13. Caprio, S., M. Bronson, R. S. Sherwin, F. Rife, & W. V. Tamborlane (1996). Co-existence of severe insulin resistance and hyperinsulinaemia in pre-adolescent obese children. *Diabetologia* 39: 1489–1497.

14. Strauss, R. S. (2000). Childhood Obesity and Self-Esteem. *Pediatrics* 105(1): 15.

15. Schwartz, M. B., & R. Puhl (2003). Childhood obesity: A societal problem to solve *Obesity Reviews* 4 (1): 57–71.

16. Lederer, E. M. Teenager takes overdose after years of 'fatty' taunts. *The Associated Press*, 1 October, 1997.

17. Popkin, B. M. (1998). The nutrition transition and its health implications in lower-income countries. *Public Health Nutr.* 1: 5–21.

18. Popkin, B. M. (2001). The nutrition transition and obesity in the developing world. *J. Nutr.* 131(3): 871S–873S.

19. Prentice, A. M. (2006). The emerging epidemic of obesity in developing countries. *Int. J. Epidemiol* 35(1): 93–99.

20. Kruger, H. S., T. Puoane, M. Senekal, & M. T. van der Merwe (2005). Obesity in South Africa: Challenges for government and health professionals. *Public Health Nutr.* 8: 491–500.

Features of successful academic writing

Your written assignments at university should:

1. express a clear, detailed and critical opinion/**stance**,

2. **cite** ideas from multiple academic sources to support that stance, and

3. be clearly and logically **organized**.

You will learn how to achieve these aspects of academic writing throughout the textbook.

Task 5
Identify features of a successful academic essay or report

Look again at the essay or report that you just read. Each text has a number of places which have been bolded and underlined. These are places where stance, organization and citation occur successfully. Make a note of **why** they are successful to the right of the text.

Task 6
Compare features of successful academic writing with your partner

Work in pairs with a student who read and analyzed the same text as you. Compare the features you found.

Homework
Identify features of a successful academic essay/report

If you completed Task 5 using the essay, read and annotate the report for features of successful academic writing.

If you completed Task 5 using the report, read and annotate the essay for features of successful academic writing.

Task 7
Identify the need for academic sources

Successful academic writing requires the incorporation of academic sources. With a partner, discuss and brainstorm why we need academic sources, where we can find them, and what makes a source suitable for academic usage.

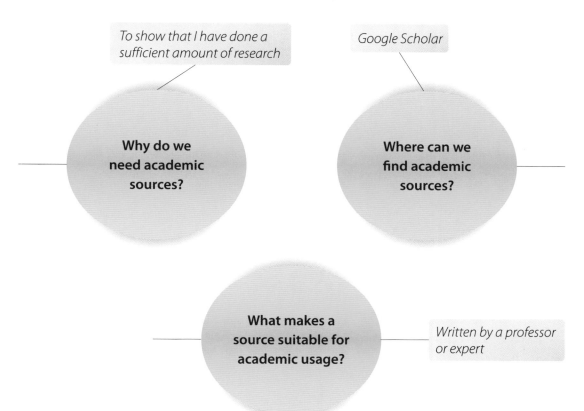

Identifying quality sources of academic information for your assignments

One important skill you will need throughout your university education is the ability to search for and select **quality academic information**. You will not be able to complete your assignments without this skill.

How do you know whether a source of information is a **quality academic source**?

Generally, information that has been through some kind of **editorial process** or has been **"fact-checked"** is reasonably reliable. It includes:

- books,

- journal articles (in print and online), and

- articles from reputable newspaper/magazine.

Even though these sources have been through an editorial process, you still need to **look for bias** on the part of the author, especially in newspaper and magazine articles. You should also think about the quality of journalism in the newspaper itself and whether it is part of the tabloid press. The sources below are very likely to be reliable, although you cannot be sure that they have been edited or fact-checked. These include:

- government publications (in print and online), and

- publications (in print and online) of well-known organizations, e.g. The World Health Organization, The World Bank, and Amnesty International.

Lastly, there is the Internet. No one needs to go through any editorial process to publish information on a website. This is why you need to be **very careful** when you use information from a website.

When using an Internet source, you should ask yourself the following questions:

1. What is the purpose of the website?

- Advocacy for a cause (change opinion)

- Commercial (sell a product or service; company websites)

- Reference (provide access to information)

2. Does the author have any qualifications related to the subject of the website?
Look for information in sections called something like "About us" or "Who we are".

3. Does the content of the website show that the information is up-to-date?
Look for dates listed.

4. Is the language used objective, or is it very emotional?
Emotional language can show that the writer is biased.

5. Is the website linked to other well-known websites?
Do the authors link their website to other well-known websites?

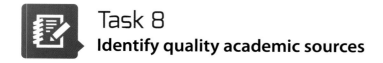

Task 8
Identify quality academic sources

Look at the seven texts below and determine whether each source is a quality academic source by filling in the chart. Justify your answers. Afterwards, compare your answers with a classmate.

Text	Good academic source?	Why or why not?
Text 1 – Book	Y/N	
Text 2 – Website	Y/N	
Text 3 – Website	Y/N	
Text 4 – Journal Article	Y/N	
Text 5 – Wikipedia	Y/N	
Text 6 – Newspaper Article	Y/N	
Text 7 – Blog Entry	Y/N	

TEXT 1
Book

The Problem of the Work-Life Balance
by Amanda Prince
Published by South Australia University Press, 2010

Longer working hours, the high unemployment rate and lack of child care are just some of the barriers to a good work-life balance. Data gathered from interviews with mothers and fathers, employers and employees shows that the employment system in Australia and New Zealand has many systematic problems (see Chan, 2011). The lack of an affordable child care system leads to a loss of hundreds of millions of dollars from the economy in lost productivity (Watson, 2010).

TEXT 2
www.naturalhealth.org.uk/aboutus

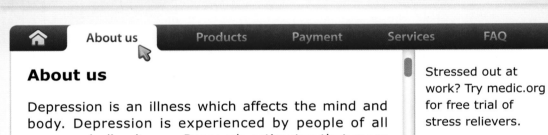

About us   Products   Payment   Services   FAQ

About us

Depression is an illness which affects the mind and body. Depression is experienced by people of all races and all cultures. Research estimates that more than 2.7 million people in the United Kingdom are currently suffering from depression. About 7,000 people commit suicide each year in the UK because of depression. Most people will experience depression at some time in their lives.

Since we began our company, we have helped thousands of people overcome depression by teaching them how to eat healthier and how to use meditation to relieve stress. We have also trained hundreds of people who work in the health care field.

Currently we have about 1,500 students studying with us from around the world. Go to our comments page to see the messages from our many satisfied customers. We currently offer over 20 courses on diet and lifestyle. We hope that you will join us and begin to lead a healthier life today.

Stressed out at work? Try medic.org for free trial of stress relievers.

Our testimonials:
"I never thought I would get rid of my depression, but GoSad worked and I now feel ready to take on the world!" (Mandy, 26, UK). To purchase GoSad, go to www.gosad.com today!

TEXT 3

Home | **Research** | Affiliations | Risks of Obesity | **About us** | Contact

Research

The link between cancer and obesity

By John Chan, PhD, published on 29 April 2009

Considerable evidence shows that being overweight or obese plays an important role in the development of certain cancers. It has been clearly associated with a 200% increased risk of kidney cancer and a 150% increased risk of breast cancer in women. It seems that there is also a strong relationship between weight and colorectal cancer, gall bladder cancer and thyroid cancer in women. There is strong evidence from animal experiments that maintaining a healthy weight can delay the onset of many cancers. More research is needed to show whether this is true in humans as well.

Donate to Environmental Research; go to www.environment.org

About us
The obesity group is a nonprofit scientific organization related to research, prevention and treatment of obesity.

The society has 2,600 members, 50% of whom have a PhD, 32% are MDs and 14% are RDs. Members work in universities, hospitals, individual or group practice, medical schools, government and other fields.

The society publishes in peer-reviewed journals and holds a yearly international conference attended by over 1,000 medical professionals each year.

TEXT 4
Journal of Environmental Pollution

Journal of Environmental Pollution 45 (2010), 104–132

Air pollution and health, by Prof. John Duggan, PhD, and Prof. Levi Whitby, MD, School of Medicine, Southampton General Hospital, Southampton, UK

Abstract

The health effects of air pollution have been the subject of extensive study in recent years. Exposure to pollutants has been associated with lower life expectancy (hypothesized to be possibly 2–3 years depending on the level of pollution) and admission to hospital as a result of respiratory and cardiovascular disease (about 3% of the population in heavily polluted cities). Negative health effects have also been seen at very low levels of exposure. In this article, the evidence for adverse effects on health of selected air pollutants is discussed.

TEXT 5
Wikipedia

Differences in access to health care in the United States

Reasons for differences in access to health care are many but can include the following:

- **Lack of insurance coverage.** Minority groups in the United States lack insurance coverage at higher rates than the majority Caucasian population. It is estimated that 19% of minority groups lack coverage, compared with 11.3% of Caucasians.

- **Structural barriers.** These barriers include poor transportation, an inability to schedule appointments quickly or during convenient hours, and excessive time spent in the waiting room, all of which affect a person's ability and willingness to obtain needed care. This is especially problematic in rural areas, where the emergency room waiting time is 4.3 hours, compared to 2.4 hours in cities.

- **Linguistic barriers.** Medical care is difficult to access for those who do not speak English. They are reluctant to seek medical help if they fear there will be no one to translate for them.

TEXT 6
California Times, Saturday, 25 July 2009

The worst-case scenario sees hundreds of thousands of deaths in the US from swine flu in the next two years, by John Williamson

Hundreds of thousands of Americans could die in the following years if a vaccine and other control measures for the new H1N1 influenza are not effective. The Center for Disease Control and Prevention (CDC) has also suggested that when the pandemic peaks, as much as 40% of the workforce could be affected.

Nineteen US states are now reporting widespread flu activity, mainly H1N1, according to Dr. John Schmidt, director of the CDC's National Center for Immunization and Respiratory Diseases. "That's very unusual at this time of year," he said. "This shows how easy it is to catch this type of virus."

Schmidt stated that in the last few months, 6% to 8% of the population in many US cities was infected by the virus even though it is not common to have figures like that in spring. Now that the winter season is coming, "we think it will reach two to three times that number." Normally, 1% to 10% of people in a community are infected with seasonal flu.

TEXT 7
www.eviloil.com/evilactsblog

Oil Empire   **Evil Acts Blog**   Stop Them   How to Help   Pics of Evil Oil

Evil Acts Blog

The oil industry is destroying our beautiful oceans and filling our skies with deadly pollution while profiting in the billions from doing this. Why do we keep allowing them to do this? Statistics definitively prove that global warming is a huge threat to our society and evil oil is the reason for it. Just look at the most recent oil spill outside the coast of America. It was a huge spill that affected over 80% of the marine population and left the ocean pitch black! If we don't do something right now, we're all going to be drowning in evil oil.

I've started this website specifically to build advocacy for stopping these evil oil companies from damaging our environment and its beauty. We've had enough and it's time we take back what belongs to us naturally. With so many viable alternative energy options such as wind and solar, why are evil oil companies still producing so much oil? Why won't they invest in these energy alternatives. Let's put a stop to this. We need to do this now because it's clear from the numbers that the situation is getting worse.

Task 9
Search for good academic sources

Your teacher will now show you how to use Google Scholar and your university's library system to search for good academic sources. Note down the five most important tips you hear.

1.

2.

3.

4.

5.

Task 10
Understand different types of supporting evidence

After evaluating sources, you need to select from a range of types of evidence. Decide whether the following statements are true or false and then check your answers with the information box below.

1. True or False	The most common form of evidence used in academic writing is expert evidence through direct quotations.
2. True or False	Common knowledge and personal accounts are often not cited and come from the writer rather than academic sources.
3. True or False	To use expert evidence through quotations, you need to change the words in the original information.
4. True or False	Statistics are a type of evidence that can stand alone and does not need any explanation or interpretation.
5. True or False	Expert evidence through paraphrasing requires quotation marks and copying the same words that are used in the original information.

Types of supporting evidence for your stance

To support your stance, you will need a range of evidence. Here are some types of evidence that you can use to back up your stance:

1. **Statistics:** Numbers and figures can help strengthen the arguments supporting your stance. However, they should not be left alone to explain themselves. You need to explain or interpret them.

2. **Expert Evidence through Quotations:** These are often used when the quoted information is from an authoritative source and contains powerful language or technical terms that you feel need to be kept in the original words. Quotes should be kept at a minimum because they are very easy to overuse, which could indicate that you have not fully understood or read your sources. The part of the original information that you want to quote needs to be copied word for word and placed in quotation marks (" . . . "). Also, never leave a quote by itself in your report or essay; always explain or interpret the quote.

3. **Expert Evidence through Paraphrasing:** This is the most common form of evidence as it shows that you have read and understood the information from your sources and that you can use your own words to summarize and integrate the original information into your arguments.

4. **Common Knowledge:** This is information that is highly likely to be known to others in the general public, your own local setting, or your academic discipline. This type of information is often not cited and can serve as background information in your introduction/conclusion or as a part of your argument that is later supported by information from an academic source. Be careful of overusing this type of evidence without support from information in academic sources.

5. **Personal Accounts:** These are often from personal observations that are not supported by research. They are generally used to support arguments with real-world examples that you know about. This type of evidence needs to be carefully and strategically combined with information from academic sources.

Task 11
Identify types of supporting evidence for your stance

The five different types of evidence are listed in the boxes below. Short excerpts from the essay and report that you read previously can also be found below. In the boxes on the right column, write the types of evidence that best match the short excerpts.

Common Knowledge   Statistics   Personal Accounts

Expert Evidence through Quotations   Expert Evidence through Paraphrasing

Short excerpt	Where can you find this?	Type of supporting evidence
One clear benefit to government funding is that those who cannot afford healthcare are provided with it.	Essay; 3rd paragraph; 2nd sentence	
The rates for one urban area in India (Amritsar in the Punjab region) were slightly lower than in urban China: 14% of boys and 18.3% of girls aged 10–15 years were found to be overweight, and of those, 5% of boys and 6.3% of girls were obese [6].	Report; Section 2; 4th paragraph	
Nonetheless, they can be used as starting points for how a combined approach to healthcare can be administered as supported by Haseltine (2013), a noted Harvard professor and AIDS researcher, who believes that an investigation of the Singaporean healthcare system should be a requisite when government officials debate issues concerning healthcare systems.	Essay; 4th paragraph; middle of paragraph	
Davis et al. (2007) report that "despite having the most costly health system in the world, the United States consistently underperforms on most dimensions of performance, relative to other countries" (p. 34).	Essay; 2nd paragraph; 3rd sentence	

Why do you think there are no examples of personal accounts in the essay/report?

Homework

Prepare for a tutorial discussion

In your first speaking tutorial, you will formulate a stance to the health-related questions below and search for two academic sources to support your stance.

1. Is there a good work-life balance in your country?

2. What are some realistic ways that work-life balance can be improved?

Read and establish your stance on the questions. As you read, take notes of the relevant supporting evidence. Be sure to include at least two different types of evidence.

ACADEMIC SPEAKING

Task 1
Consider the purpose of university tutorial discussions

Step 1: What do you think is the main purpose of university tutorial discussions? Spend a few minutes discussing this question with two to three students.

Step 2: Now read what some professors and tutors said when they were asked about the purpose of a tutorial discussion. Which purposes did they mention that you didn't think of in Step 1?

"I think that by sharing information with others, students are challenged to think about topics in new ways and to practise critical thinking skills. This can help them gain a deeper understanding of academic issues."

"Tutorial discussions give students a reason to go and research a topic. If they don't do this, they may let both themselves and the group down . . . so that's a strong motivator. I think without putting in the time reading, it's hard for students to understand complex topics."

"In tutorials, students have to work together to solve problems. I think this process helps them build confidence and interpersonal skills they will need later in life. I wish we'd had tutorial discussions when I was at university!"

"I feel that tutorial discussions are a great opportunity for students to think about their progress during the course. They can apply what they learnt in the lecture and the tutor has a chance to see how his or her students are progressing and give them the feedback they need."

"You know, in tutorial discussions you can't hide like you can in a lecture. You have to be active . . . both when you prepare and in class. By doing the research yourself and then discussing it, I think you're much more likely to remember what you've learnt than if you just listen passively . . . discussions make learning more memorable."

Discuss the following two questions with your classmates:

1. How might university discussions differ in purpose from discussions you have participated in before at school?

2. What do you think will be the biggest challenges for you in adapting to university discussions?

Task 2
Analyze discussion feedback

Read the following examples of discussion feedback from a tutor in a university English class. Using three different colours, highlight what the students **did well**, what they still need to **improve** and what the **tutor's advice** is on how they could improve.

Feedback for Student 1:

"You prepared well for this tutorial and made some effective notes. This helped you give some relevant examples to support your stance. Do you realize that you look down at your notes a lot though and that you speak very quickly, which can make it difficult to follow you? Don't forget to look at the other students as you speak and go a little slower. Perhaps you could ask questions occasionally to check students are with you."

Feedback for Student 2:

"You approached this tutorial seriously, were well-informed and did a good job of citing your sources clearly. I sometimes found it hard though to identify your stance. Remember, you shouldn't be trying to say everything you know, you need to be more selective. Practise recording your ideas in note form and organize them by topic and not the text. This way it should be easier for others to follow your position and to respond to you."

Feedback for Student 3:

"Well done. You managed to speak more loudly and clearly this time; you also made better eye contact and appeared more confident. I think you could disagree (politely) more and generally, be more critical of what you hear. Before the next discussion you might find it helpful to imagine what other people might say to help you consider alternative ideas and perspectives."

Feedback for Student 4:

"I noticed you balanced agreement and disagreement well this time, but I'm not sure that all your turns link properly to what the previous speaker said, e.g. if a question is asked, answer it first and then add your own stance, and if you change the topic, signal this too. You are using a good range of vocabulary, but you often forget to use modals and adverbs to state opinions cautiously, e.g. 'New students *might/ perhaps* need some time to adapt.'"

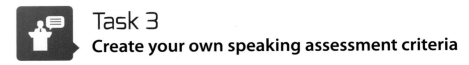

Task 3
Create your own speaking assessment criteria

Look at Task 1 and Task 2 again, what do you now think the distinguishing features of a successful university discussion are? In groups of three to four, create **four university discussion assessment criteria**. Record them in the table below, adding one or two examples for each criterion. The first has been done for you as an example.

University Discussion Assessment Criteria	
Criterion 1: Stance **Example:** *It is **clear and concise**. This means that I should express only one idea at a time and I should also change the written language to simple, spoken language.* **Example:** *There is **critical thought**. This means that I should show an awareness of different views, i.e. the complexity of academic argument.*	**Criterion 2:** **Example:** **Example:**
Criterion 3: **Example:** **Example:**	**Criterion 4:** **Example:** **Example:**

Task 4
Participate in a tutorial discussion

Now, hold a 30-minute tutorial discussion with your group members. The topic of your discussion addresses the following questions:

    1. Is there a good work-life balance in your country?

    2. What are some realistic ways that work-life balance could be improved?

Task 5
Analyze your strengths and weaknesses

Take five minutes to fill in the form below. Rate your overall performance on each criterion as follows:

1 = I did this **most of the time**   **2** = I did this **some of the time**   **3** = I **rarely** did this

My stance was: **clear** – e.g. I changed the written language in the source to my own spoken language. **concise** – e.g. I expressed one idea at a time. **critical** – e.g. I acknowledged that academic ideas are complex, not black and white.	1 ☐ 2 ☐ 3 ☐ 1 ☐ 2 ☐ 3 ☐ 1 ☐ 2 ☐ 3 ☐
I interacted well by: **linking my ideas smoothly into the discussion** – e.g. I linked my point to a point that had been mentioned before. **using active listening skills** – e.g. I used eye contact, nodding and expressions of agreement. **not dominating** – e.g. I allowed other students to break into the discussion.	1 ☐ 2 ☐ 3 ☐ 1 ☐ 2 ☐ 3 ☐ 1 ☐ 2 ☐ 3 ☐
My language was: **fluent** – e.g. I was able to speak without a lot of hesitations. **accurate** – e.g. I was able to use a range of grammar and vocabulary to express complex academic ideas. **clear** – e.g. I used stress, intonation and pausing to express my meaning.	1 ☐ 2 ☐ 3 ☐ 1 ☐ 2 ☐ 3 ☐ 1 ☐ 2 ☐ 3 ☐
I cited: **from sources to support my stance** – e.g. I didn't just rely on my own personal opinion in the discussion. **by mentioning the reliability of my source** – e.g. I mentioned that the information I cited came from a reliable source (*The Journal of XX*/The World Health Organization).	1 ☐ 2 ☐ 3 ☐ 1 ☐ 2 ☐ 3 ☐

Ideas for future improvement

2
GLOBAL ISSUES

Note-taking and paraphrasing

Learning outcomes

By the end of this unit, you should be able to:

- analyze assignment topics,
- take notes from sources within a plan,
- synthesize ideas through note-taking and paraphrasing,
- reference multiple sources concurrently to strengthen evidence relating to your stance,
- use linking words and phrases to show the relationship between arguments and counter-arguments, and
- transform written language into spoken language during a tutorial discussion.

ACADEMIC WRITING

 ## Task 1
Achieve the Millennium Development Goals

In the year 2000, eight international development goals were established following the Millennium Summit of the United Nations. These goals, shown below, aim to encourage development in the world's poorest countries by improving social and economic conditions.

Work in groups of three and choose one of the above Millennium Development Goals. Imagine you are policy-makers in a developing country who have just been given $1 million by an aid agency to promote your Millennium Development Goal.

In your group, discuss how you would spend this money. Then choose a note taker to record your ideas or plan of action in the space below.

Our Millennium Development Goal:

Task 2
Prioritize economic or human development

Share your plan of action with other groups and, using the table below, write two ideas which you feel will have the biggest impact in each category. An example has been done for you.

Plans which mainly develop the economy	Plans which mainly develop human well-being
• Initiate a training programme which promotes ecotourism (environmental sustainability) • •	• Run awareness programmes for midwives in rural areas (maternal health) • •

Plans which develop both the economy and human well-being

• Deliver a women's agricultural project in rural areas (gender equality)

•

•

Now, drawing on these ideas, decide which you believe is more important when aiming to achieve the Millennium Development Goals: economic or human development.

Based on these ideas, I think that human/economic development is more important when aiming to achieve the Millennium Development Goals.

The importance of understanding an assignment topic

Recall from the previous unit that the academic writing process begins with a search for a range of information on the topic from different viewpoints.

However, before you are able to begin this search, it is necessary for you to ensure that you fully understand the assignment topic so that you can read selectively and critically.

 ## Task 3
Analyze an assignment topic

Imagine you are asked to write a report on the following topic, which relates to your discussion in the preceding tasks:

> **Compare and contrast Human Capital Theory and the Capabilities Approach and evaluate which has a more positive impact on society.**

Look at the five steps in the left column below which can help you prepare for the writing process. Then complete the gaps in the right column. When you are finished with each step, compare your answers with a partner.

Steps in analyzing an assignment topic	Application of these steps to a given topic
1: Circle the directive verbs and think about what they ask you to do.	Compare and contrast Human Capital Theory and the Capabilities Approach and evaluate which has a more positive impact on society. • *Compare* and *contrast* ask you to _____ _____ . • *Evaluate* asks you to _____ _____ .

2: Underline the main content words and think about what they mean.	Compare and contrast Human Capital Theory and the Capabilities Approach and evaluate which has a more positive impact on society. • _____ • _____ • _____
3: Think about what kind of information you will need to find in order to complete the assignment.	Use the information you generated in Steps 1 and 2 to help you complete this step. You will need to find: • *a range of sources which define the key terms in the report topic;* • _____ • _____ • _____
4: Develop an outline for the report.	There is no one correct way of doing this. However, you need to ensure that the structure of your report will help you answer the assignment topic fully. Use your notes above to develop an outline for this report. You may wish to add subheadings or reduce/increase the number of headings given below: 1. Introduction 2. _____ 3. _____ 4. _____ 5. _____ 6. _____ These headings will help you synthesize ideas later during the note-taking stage of the writing process.
5: Think about what kind of texts would have the information you need to support your stance in an academic way.	This kind of information is likely to be found in: • *United Nations websites* • *NGO websites* • _____ • _____ • _____ • _____

If you were required to complete this assignment, you would now be ready to begin the reading/note-taking process.

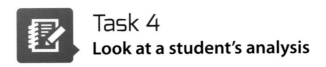

Task 4
Look at a student's analysis

This assignment was completed by another student, Katie. Look at pages 154 and 155 to see how she analyzed the assignment topic. Take a moment to compare her analysis to your own.

The process of note-taking

As you develop a deeper understanding of the topic through reading, you will continuously refine your notes by:

- adding/removing/changing headings,
- clustering related concepts,
- replacing weak evidence with stronger examples,
- expanding on evidence with related references, and
- integrating your stance into your notes.

This process is illustrated in the figure below:

Task 5

Take notes within a plan

Look at the following two versions of Katie's notes. It is clear that the first version was drafted early on in the note-taking process described above, while the second version was developed after much refinement.

Notice, at this stage, that some of the notes are incomplete. You will complete these later, in Task 8.

Version 1

	HCT	CA
Defn./ background		• <u>Capabilities Approach:</u> ≠ HCT, ∴ CA supports focus of investment in areas which ↑ human well-being rather than economic growth. • Looks @ developing humans' capabilities

Pros	• Investment in ppl can → economic growth → more economic benefits
	• Easy to model & quantify spending
	  ○ ∴ perceived as practical by donor agencies
		• Human development is foregrounded over economic growth
		  ○ ∴ aid more likely to ↑ well-being
		• Developing capabilities→ ↑ achievement of things ppl want to do
		• Development more equitable
		• Ppl have greater control over their environments

Cons	• Simplistic ∴ cannot really model returns
	• Doesn't account for impact on gender/ well-being
	  ○ ∴ investment could ↓ overall well-being
	  ○ ∴ could be unethical	

Version 2

Aid in a Globalizing World: economic or human development?

1 **1. Introduction**

2 **2. Theories underpinning allocation of development aid**

3   • Incl brief intro to structure of this section

4 **2.1 Economic growth in Human Capital Theory (HCT)**

5   • In past: investment in technology → economic growth . . . now

6   • HCT believes investing in ppl → economic growth

7   ○ E.g. $$ allocated to education can ↑ economy after some time

8   • Policymakers ☺ eco. growth

9   ○ ∴ p'makers often adopt HCT when making decisions

10   • Uses "rate of return" as a measurement tool

11   (Okene, 2006)

12   **2.1.1 The shortcomings of relying on Human Capital Theory**

13   • Seems simplistic . . . some of my thoughts on/responses to

14   ideas in 2.1:

15   ○ What about the nature of edu?/gender?/Will the edu

16   actually be used?

17   • Could aid actually cause more harm!!?

18 **2.2 Human development in the Capabilities Approach (CA)**

19   • Human dev. more important than eco dev. here (Sen, 1979;

20   Nussbaum & Sen, 1993; Robeyns, 2005; OECD, 2006)

21   • HCT uses GDP (output-based) but CA uses HDI, GEM, and GII (see

22   UNDP site for details)

23   • " . . . while income is generally an important means to well-being

24   and freedom, it can only serve as a rough proxy for what intrinsically

25   matters, namely people's capabilities" (Robeyns, 2005, p97)

26   • What about issues in 2.1.1? Flesh out eg on an agricultural project for

27   women v computer training for men in ?Afghanistan.*Look into this further

28   **2.2.1 The importance of developing appropriate human capabilities**

29   • BUT Potential issue: How do we know what capabilities are

30   important in a society?

31   • Do policymakers know what → well-being?

32   ○ ∴ Nussbaum (2000) [in Newman (2002)] made a list of 10

33   main capabilities (see source for egs)

34 **3. Merits of foregrounding human development**

35   • Despite challenges of CA in 2.2.1, its focus on ppl more likely →

36   well-being than HCT's focus on econ.

37   • Draw on issues of HCT in 2.1.1 to show how wrong aid → harm

38   • Show how pros of CA in 2.2 contrast problematic HCT ito ethics &

39   sustainability.

With a partner, discuss the following questions:

1. Is Katie's stance similar/different from the viewpoint you established at the end of Task 2? How do you know?

2. What are some similarities and differences between the first and the second versions of Katie's notes?

Task 6
Take notes effectively

Look again at Katie's notes in Task 5 and, on your own, answer the questions below. Include the line number of an example from the notes to support your ideas.

	Question	My thoughts	Line number from notes
Noting sources	1. Do all the ideas in the notes come from the sources? Why/why not?		
	2. Why are some of the sources paraphrased and not direct quotes?		
	3. How are direct quotes incorporated?		
	4. Why is there more than one source under each heading?		
	5. What reference details are included in the notes?		
	6. Why is this the case?		
Synthesizing ideas	7. Are the notes grouped according to sources or according to themes?		
	8. What role do the headings play in helping the note-taker synthesize ideas?		
	9. How are the relationships between the main and supporting ideas conveyed in the notes?		

	10. How will synthesizing ideas at the note-taking stage help the writer during the writing stage?		
	11. How is the complexity of the topic acknowledged in the notes?		
	12. Why is this important?		
	13. What language is used in the notes to show the relationship between ideas?		
	14. What symbols are used in the notes to show the relationship between ideas?		
	15. What role do bulleting and indentation play?		
	16. Which sections of the report contain no specific notes? Why?		
Incorporating stance	17. How is the note-taker's stance incorporated into the notes?		
	18. Why does the writer do this at the note-taking stage?		

Task 7

Develop a note-taking checklist

Now share your answers to Task 6 with three other classmates and develop your own "Note-taking Checklist" below. To complete this task, you will need to:

- decide which are the eight most important aspects of note-taking inspected in Task 6, through negotiation with your group members,

- create your own subcategories for your checklist based on the key ideas you select, and

- personalize your checklist to address your own needs.

Note-taking Checklist			
Subcategory	#	I have . . .	Partner's assessment in Task 8 (tick if present ✓)
Use of symbols	e.g.	. . . used symbols to speed up the note-taking process.	
	1		
	2		
	3		
	4		
	5		
	6		
	7		
	8		

Task 8
Develop a note-taking style

Now that you have developed a checklist, you are ready to practise your own note-taking skills. In order to do this,

1. look below at two of the sources used by Katie, and

2. complete Version 1 of Katie's notes in Task 5 by drawing on these source texts.

A

What constitutes "a capability" has recently received much attention in aid agencies and governments of both developed and developing nations. Several attempts to index capabilities and their relationship to human well-being have proven popular; most notably, the United Nations' Human Development Index (HDI).

However, many argue that identifying what constitutes well-being is a nearly impossible challenge, and, by extension, establishing which capabilities to foster is often an overwhelming task for policymakers. Notwithstanding the above difficulties, Nussbaum (2000) argues for ten basic principles which have the potential to greatly assist decision-making in democratic environments. These principles therefore offer a useful framework for the achievement of the overarching capabilities applicable to all human beings:

1. the ability to live
2. the ability to have bodily health
3. the ability to have bodily integrity and freedom of movement
4. the ability to use one's senses, imagination, and thought
5. the ability to have attachments and authentic emotions
6. the ability to know the difference between good and bad
7. the ability to affiliate with whom one wishes
8. the ability to live with concern for other species
9. the ability to play
10. the ability to have control over one's environment

(Newman, 2002)

A feature fundamental to Human Capital Theory is the role played by people in the development of economic growth, a chief objective of aid for policymakers adopting this approach. This theory positions humans as technology was positioned in the past: investing in technology (or human capital in this case) has the potential to lead to economic returns. For instance, a national investment in free higher education or a regional endowment in a health and nutrition campaign has the potential to yield economic benefits.

Consider the example of free higher education for a moment. In the instance that the costs associated with this intervention exceed the benefits, the rate of return to investment would be negative and thus, the investment would be deemed unwise within the HCT paradigm. This may occur in a country with high levels of graduate unemployment, for example. Policymakers would then find alternative ways to allocate their resources which would yield a positive rate of return.

(Okene, 2006)

When you have finished taking notes,

1. swap your notes with a partner,

2. use your partner's checklist in Task 7 to assess their notes, and

3. return your feedback to your partner.

Now look at Katie's full set of notes on page 156. Compare the way she has taken notes with the way you and your partner have completed this task. Take a moment to reflect on/improve the checklist you created in Task 7.

 ## Task 9
Develop a full draft

Read the full draft of Katie's report below and decide whether the following statements are true or false.

Statement	True/False?
Katie believes that allocating aid towards human development is more important than allocating it towards economic development.	
Katie believes economic development is likely to be one of several aspects which promote well-being.	
Katie offers an example to help explain the Capabilities Approach.	
Katie has written a "forward-looking" conclusion.	

Aid in a Globalizing World: Economic or Human Development?

1. Introduction

In 2000, the United Nations established the eight Millennium Development Goals (MDGs), which aim to enhance efforts of member states in assisting countries and regions facing health, wealth, equality, and environmental challenges. The target date for achieving these goals is 2015; a worrying deadline given that more than half of the indicators associated with the MDGs reveal that progress is insufficient to reach the target (UN, 2012). This troubling mismatch between the forecasted and actual progress in international development highlights the importance of exploring approaches adopted when nations and agencies decide how aid is allocated and the consequent impact on societies. This report briefly outlines two popular approaches: Human Capital Theory (HCT), which places economic growth as the main objective of development aid, and the Capabilities Approach (CA), which places human well-being as its key aim. This will provide a platform to argue that aid should focus on human well-being rather than economic growth in order to have an optimal impact on society as a whole.

2. Theories underpinning allocation of development aid

The following sections briefly explore the theory behind these two popular but somewhat conflicting approaches to how donor agencies and policymakers allocate development aid.

2.1 Economic growth in Human Capital Theory (HCT)

Despite the inclusion of the word "human" in the term, HCT in fact foregrounds economic growth as the core objective of development. Within this approach, it is believed that investing in people, through education, health and nutrition for example, will lead to economic benefits for individuals and society (Okene, 2006). This investment in people is termed "human capital" and the economic benefits derived from investing in this human capital are calculated as a rate of return.

Decisions regarding whether to invest in developing higher-education systems within a country, for example, are therefore based on the rate of economic return. In other words, policymakers ask themselves the following question, "Will a given amount of public investment in higher-education resources yield a greater amount of returns in labour market productivity and worker earnings?" If the answer is "Yes", investment is justified within the HCT paradigm.

2.1.1 The shortcomings of relying on HCT

While this approach appears to be practical to many donor agencies and government bodies, its assumption that development can be measured and modelled as a rate of return is, in most cases, simplistic. This can be illustrated through the example of Afghanistan. Each dollar spent on education in this nation is likely to yield greater productivity in the labour market and is consequently likely to encourage investment in education. However, if this education is only accessible to certain sections of society or favours males over females, its impact on the distribution of wealth or gender equality may be negative. Thus, while investment in education leads to economic growth, society's well-being as a whole may be harmed as a result of the nature of the investment. Aid which causes more harm than good is clearly counterproductive if not unethical and places HCT's "economic focus" in a questionable light.

2.2 Human development in the Capabilities Approach (CA)

An alternative approach to deciding how resources are allocated is the CA. This approach repositions economic development as one means of human development and acknowledges that there are many social, moral and cultural issues not accounted for in HCT (Sen, 1979; Nussbaum & Sen, 1993; Robeyns, 2005; OECD, 2006). Robeyns, a key proponent of the CA, convincingly argues that, "while income is generally an important means to well-being and freedom, it can only serve as a rough proxy for what intrinsically matters, namely people's capabilities" (Robeyns, 2005, p. 97). Capabilities, in this context, are skills which are developed through goods and services (e.g. education) and a range of social contexts (e.g. environmental factors or cultural norms) which result in an individual's ability to do things he/she wishes to do (Sen, 1979; Robeyns, 2005; Nussbaum, 2000). Here, the main objective is not to stimulate economic growth but create society capable of achieving things which enhance its well-being.

Returning to the example of investment in education in Afghanistan noted in Section 2.1.1, the CA would aim to foster a schooling system which equitably develops capabilities which the people going through the system perceive as likely to enhance their well-being. For instance, a women's agricultural training programme may yield lower economic returns than a course on computer technology for men but may lead to a greater sense of well-being for society as a whole. In this instance, women become more empowered, have greater control over their environments, and are more likely to use their generated income to enhance the health and well-being of their (male and female) children.

The CA clearly moves beyond HCT's use of output-based measures such as GDP by using more humane indices of progress, including the Human Development Index, the Gender Empowerment Measure, and the Gender Inequality Index. These indices aim to embody a broad range of capabilities and are used as tools by many aid agencies, such as the UN, to inform how development aid should be spent.

2.2.1 The importance of developing appropriate human capabilities

An associated challenge with the CA is selecting which capability sets are most in need of development in a given context. Nussbaum (2000) and Newman (2002) controversially argue for a general list of ten central human capabilities, including freedom of senses, imagination and thought; choice of affiliation; control over one's environment; and bodily health. Critics of the CA may note that developing capability sets relies on policymakers' thorough understanding of what citizens in a given society consider "well-being". For example, the need to develop imagination and thought in the education system may be more pressing in a society with a heavily censored press than in a nation with strong freedom of speech. Thus, while Nussbaum's list of central human capabilities serves as a useful starting point for aid allocation, adopting a "one size fits all" approach is clearly suboptimal.

3. Merits of foregrounding human development

Despite the challenges of identifying which capabilities a society wants and needs, a focus on human development is more likely to enhance well-being than an emphasis on economic growth, as shown in sections 2.1.1 and 2.2. HCT's focus on economic growth may also very well overlook fundamental gender equality issues or environmental sustainability concerns. In the worst-case scenario, economic development of this kind could potentially diminish a society's overall well-being, placing development aid in a very questionable light.

On the other hand, as discussed in Section 2.2, the CA empowers humans rather than only economies by aiming to develop capability sets which provide individuals and societies with the opportunities to function in areas which drive sustainable human well-being. This paradigm, which focuses on enhancing the capability and agency of humans irrespective of the rate of economic return, therefore appears to be (i) more ethical, as it acknowledges cultural and personal preference; and (ii) more sustainable, as agents have ownership over the choices they make and environmental sustainability is considered within the approach.

4. Conclusion

The above sections have endeavoured to illustrate that the choice of approach when allocating aid has a significant impact on the nature of development. HCT's prioritization of economic growth at the potential expense of human development seems short-sighted, especially when the more holistic CA may include economic development as one of several aspects which promote well-being in society. In view of the declining amount of international aid being offered and the imminent deadline for the achievement of the MDGs, there is a crucial need for donor agencies and policymakers to reconsider the ethics and sustainability of investment in order to develop societies, rather than solely economies.

5. References

1. Newman, A. (2002). Human Development and Capabilities. *Journal of the Development of Humanity*, 22(1): 55–20.
2. Nussbaum, M. (2000). Woman and Human Development. In S. Deneulin & L. Shahani, *An Introduction to the Human Development and Capability Approach*. London: Earthscan.
3. Nussbaum, Martha C. and Amartya Sen, eds. (1993). *The Quality of Life*. Oxford: Clarendon Press.
4. OECD. (2006). Alternative measures of well-being. *Economic Policy Reforms: Going for Growth*, pp. 129–142.

(The remaining references have been taken out to save space.)

Avoiding plagiarism when paraphrasing

Using the exact words in the original sources without any acknowledgements or quotation marks is plagiarism, a serious academic offence. To avoid this, you must rewrite (or paraphrase) the ideas in your own words. Although this takes more time, the benefits of paraphrasing are that you can show you have understood the ideas and are able to present them in your own voice.

Task 10
Move from source texts to a paraphrase

As Katie writes her first draft, she needs to paraphrase. Take a look at the following example of where Katie has paraphrased and draw lines connecting the ideas in the original source with Katie's paraphrase. An example has been done for you.

Compare your answers with a partner and discuss any differences in your thinking. When you have finished, look at page 158 and, if necessary, make changes to your original annotations.

Source text	Final version of Katie's notes	Paraphrased excerpt from Katie's report

A feature fundamental to Human Capital Theory is the role played by people in the development of economic growth, a chief objective of aid for policymakers adopting this approach. This theory positions humans as technology was positioned in the past: investing in technology (or humans in this case) has the potential to lead to economic returns. For instance, a national investment in free higher education or a regional endowment in a health and nutrition campaign has the potential to yield economic benefits. Consider the example of free higher education for a moment. In the instance that the costs associated with this intervention exceed the benefits, the rate of return to investment would be negative and thus, the investment would be deemed unwise within the HCT paradigm. This may occur in a country with high levels of graduate unemployment, for example. Policymakers would then find alternative ways to allocate their resources which would yield a positive rate of return. (Okene, 2006)	**2.1 Economic growth in Human Capital Theory (HCT)**
	 • Ppl "invested in" = Human Capital
	 • Investing in ppl (e.g. edu/health/nutrition) → economic benefit for ind and society (Okene, 2006)
	 • Returns on these ppl = rate of return (RoR) . . .
	   o this RoR ∴influences decision making
	   o e.g. if investing in edu → labour market productivity then investment is ☺ (Okene, 2006)
		2.1 Economic growth in Human Capital Theory (HCT)
		
		 Despite the inclusion of the word "human" in the term, HCT in fact foregrounds economic growth as the core objective of development. Within this approach, it is believed that investing in people, through education, health and nutrition for example, will lead to economic benefits for individuals and society (Okene, 2006). This investment in people is termed "human capital" and the economic benefits derived from investing in this human capital are calculated as a rate of return.
		
		 Decisions regarding whether to invest in developing higher-education systems within a country, for example, are therefore based on the rate of economic return. In other words, policymakers ask themselves the following question, "Will a given amount of public investment in higher-education resources yield a greater amount of returns in labour market productivity and worker earnings?" If the answer is "Yes", investment is justified within the HCT paradigm.

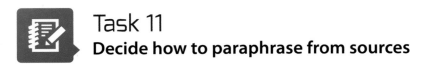

Task 11
Decide how to paraphrase from sources

The following checklist provides some useful guidelines when moving from your notes to your full draft. Use the checklist to identify these features of paraphrasing in Katie's notes/report in Task 10.

Checklist
Check that you have not plagiarized or conveyed ideas from the source text incorrectly.
Include the author and the year of publication but . . .
. . . omit the page number(s) of the source text unless you are directly quoting.
Use your own words; not those of the original text.
Retain the original meaning intended by the author.
Ensure that you make sufficient changes to the grammatical structure or items of vocabulary to avoid plagiarism.
If possible, reference multiple authors who share the same view(s) to strengthen your argument.

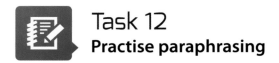

Task 12
Practise paraphrasing

Complete the following sentence:

Globalization leads to . . .

Compare your sentence with a partner, then read the text on page 51 and check your ideas.

Globalization leads to countries being more connected and interdependent culturally, economically and politically. Economically, it has led to an enormous increase in international trade and investment across different countries, resulting in an increase in wealth and living standards for many countries. For example, the average yearly income per person in China rose from US$1,460 in 1980 to US$4,120 in 1999 (Malan, 2008). However, the gap between the richest and the poorest around the world has increased from 30 to 1 in 1960 to 82 to 1 in 1995 (Purdue, 2004). Not all countries, or people within those countries, benefit from globalization equally. In many developing countries, Western companies are maximizing profits by using the cheap labour and raw materials (Kennett, 2012). Globalization often benefits the Western companies, not the people in developing countries.

Primary source: Houston, A. (2010). Has globalization improved the living standards in the third world? In S. Edward (ed.), *Globalization and Its Effects in the World* (pp. 15–23). London: Johnson Publication.

Now complete the paragraph below by paraphrasing the above text.

There are both advantages and disadvantages to globalization. According to ....

....

....

....

....

 ## Task 13
Identify appropriate paraphrasing

There are excerpts of students' writing on page 52, which contain paraphrases of the text in Task 12. Decide whether they are good or poor examples of paraphrasing. Then compare your ideas with a partner and note a reason for your answer.

Excerpt 1

Countries are now being more connected and interdependent culturally, economically and politically because of globalization. Economically, it has brought about an enormous increase in international trade and investment across different countries, leading to an increase in wealth and living standards for many countries. For instance, the average yearly income per person in China rose from $1460 USD in 1980 to $4120 in 1999.

☐ **Well paraphrased**   ☐ **Poorly paraphrased**

Reason:

Excerpt 2

Globalization has improved the economy of some developing countries. An example is China, where average incomes have increased by more than half in just two decades (Houston, 2010) as a result of increased trade with and investment by foreign companies. This essay aims to examine the relationships between international trade and the economic growth of China in the past few decades.

☐ **Well paraphrased**   ☐ **Poorly paraphrased**

Reason:

Excerpt 3

Globalization often benefits Western companies, not the people in developing countries. The reason is that in many developing countries, Western companies are maximizing profits by using the cheap labour and raw materials (Kennett, 2012 in Houston, 2010). This essay will demonstrate that not all countries, or people within those countries, benefit from globalization equally.

☐ **Well paraphrased**   ☐ **Poorly paraphrased**

Reason:

Task 14
Improve your paraphrase

Based on the aspects of paraphrasing discussed in Tasks 11 and 13, improve your paraphrase in Task 12.

Now, swap your writing with a partner and note a few comments explaining:

- strengths of the paraphrase, and

- ways in which the paraphrase could be improved.

Refer to page 160 to see an example of how you could have paraphrased the source text. Compare this paraphrase to your own. Which do you prefer? Why?

Homework
Prepare for a tutorial discussion

The topic for your next speaking tutorial is:

> **Is the impact of globalization positive or negative? Support your viewpoint by synthesizing a range of appropriate evidence.**

1. Search for information on Google Scholar and your library's electronic databases for at least two written texts on this issue.

2. Read the texts. Take notes as you read. Use the note-taking checklist developed earlier to guide the way in which you take your notes. Your peers will use this checklist to analyze your notes in the next class.

3. Make a note of the references of your source texts.

ACADEMIC
SPEAKING

Task 1
Revise note-taking

Earlier in this unit, you spent some time developing a personalized note-taking checklist. Take a moment to explain your checklist to a partner and identify similarities and differences.

Now swap the notes which you took for today's speaking tutorial with the same partner, and complete the following three steps:

1. Use your partner's note-taking checklist to assess how well he or she has taken notes.

2. Give your partner constructive feedback.

3. Explain to your partner how he or she could improve their notes in the next speaking tutorial. Give reasons for your suggestions.

Task 2
Transform written language into spoken language

Work in pairs. Student A: read the text in the box on page 55 about transforming written language into spoken language. Student B: close your book and do not read the text.

Now, Student A: explain what you have read to Student B. Together, think of another reason why it may be important to transform written language to spoken language in a tutorial discussion.

Transforming written language into spoken language

In tutorials, you are expected to present and discuss both facts and opinions about a particular topic. To do so, you need to read academic texts for your discussion.

When it comes to the tutorials, students often make the mistake of reading aloud from the sources they have read. This is problematic as reading aloud does not require that you understand the meaning behind the source and often the content is too dense for listeners to understand in real-time. It also means that your spoken style will be inconsistent and your intonation is likely to sound unnatural.

It is therefore very important to transform written language into spoken language by gaining an understanding of the information before presenting the ideas and data in the tutorial.

Task 3
An example of transforming written language into spoken language

In her search for information for the upcoming tutorial discussion, Katie came across the concept of "protectionism". She feels that this term is important to her tutorial discussion and decides to take notes on its definition in order to integrate it into her discussion of the impact of globalization on developing economies.

Look at the following two texts which define the term "protectionism". One of the texts is the original written version and the other is Katie's spoken version. As you read, decide whether Katie has accurately represented the information in the source text.

Written text	Spoken text
"Protectionism refers to the imposition of barriers to international trade by government entities. These barriers usually involve either taxes on imports — that is, tariffs — or quantitative restrictions limiting the volume of legally allowable imports of particular goods — or quotas — to achieve various economic and political targets." (p. 247) Source: *Globalization: Encyclopedia of Trade, Labour and Politics, Volume 1*	Sometimes players in the government place barriers on international trade for economic or political reasons. There are two typical examples: the first is taxing, and the second is limiting imports. These taxes are called tariffs and the limitations are called quotas. And, when tariffs or quotas are imposed, it is called protectionism.

notes

Does the spoken text accurately represent the information in the source text? ☐ Yes ☐ No

Task 4
Identify the differences between spoken and written texts

Spend a few minutes brainstorming the differences between the two texts on page 55 in terms of the categories below. An example has been done for you.

Categories	Written text	Spoken text
Grammatical structures	• Complex grammatical structures are often used.	• Complex grammatical structures are usually simplified to enhance understandability.
Vocabulary		
Signposting		
Emphasis		
Audience		

Compare your answers with a partner and then add to your notes by looking at the suggested answers on page 160.

Task 5
Prepare to transform written language into spoken language

With a partner, briefly discuss the following two questions:

1. What form of government exists in your country?

2. How does this impact on society?

On pages 57 and 58 are definitions of different forms of government around the globe. Identify **one** text and transform it from written language to spoken language.

Make concise notes below in point form (do not write out a script; you would just be putting the text back into writing). Refer to your notes in the preceding task.

Notes:

TEXT 1
Monarchy

A monarchy is a governmental system in which sovereignty of a state is held by one single person, the monarch, who is considered to be the permanent head of state. Monarchy originated in the 16th century when new nation-states were formed. The notion that the monarch represented the rule of God formed the basis of unlimited power endowed on him and his inheriting successors, a system referred to as absolute monarchy. The term has, however, evolved to include a political system in which the hereditary head of state acts as a symbolic head, as his power is confined by a constitution that mostly employs a parliamentary system headed by a prime minister. This form of government is called constitutional monarchy, as typified by the monarchy in the United Kingdom.

Source: *The Encyclopedia of Political and Social Sciences, Volume 1*, p. 76.

TEXT 2
Communism

The term "Communism" was originally used to refer to a social movement advocating the collective ownership of all means and outcomes of production by everyone in society, culminating in the abolition of class and state. Resources and manufactured products are distributed equally among all members of society, and political and economic decisions are made collectively by means of free participation of every member of society. In modern usage, the term is often used to refer to the government of a state by a Communist party, which typifies the rule of a single party centrally planning the economy and owning all means of production such as state-controlled factories. Current examples of this are China, North Korea, Cuba and Vietnam, although they do vary in their extent of adherence to communist ideology.

Source: Williamson, T. (1995). *Economic Politics: The Rise of Communism*. Camford: Camford University Press, p. 59.

TEXT 3
Democratic Socialism

The latest edition of *Webster's Third New International Dictionary* defines "socialism" as a political theory that "advocates collective or governmental ownership and administration of the means of production and distribution of goods". The term is often used in contrast to "capitalism", which "advocates private ownership for the administration of the means of production and distribution of goods". The dictionary defines a "social democrat" as "one who advocates a gradual and peaceful transition from capitalism to socialism by democratic means". Volume XV of the *Oxford English Dictionary* defines "democratic socialism" as "a socialist system achieved by democratic means" and a "social democrat" is "a member of a political party having socialistic views".

Source: Roberts, M. (2002). Democratic socialism: A note on terminology. *Current Sociology*, 22(4): 6.

TEXT 4
Capitalism

Capitalism is an economic system in which the means of production are owned and operated by private businesses for the purpose of generating profits. The supply of and demand for goods are wholly determined by a free market in which governmental intervention is kept to a minimum. Profits belong to owners who invest in businesses, and wages are paid to workers. Prices of goods and wages for workers are driven by market forces. There are two main benefits to such a system. First, it encourages competition, which in turn drives prices down. Second, it provides incentive for participation in economic activities and development.

Source: Roberts, J. (1999). *Macroeconomics*. Boston: International Press, p. 52.

Task 6

Practise transforming written language into spoken language

Work in a group with members who read about the other three forms of government.

Imagine that you are in a tutorial discussion about the merits/weaknesses of different forms of government. Your group's task is to:

1. explain the forms of government, and

2. evaluate the forms of government.

Now consider whose explanation was clearest and why. Take a few notes below and then share your feedback with other members of the group.

Taking the feedback given to you into account, repeat the above task with another group.

Task 7

Participate in a tutorial discussion

Now, hold a 30-minute tutorial discussion with your group members. The topic of your discussion is:

> **Is the impact of globalization positive or negative?**

Remember to support your viewpoint by synthesizing a range of appropriate evidence.

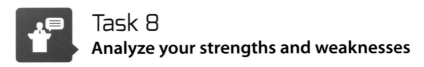

Task 8
Analyze your strengths and weaknesses

Take five minutes to fill in the form below. Rate your overall performance on each criterion as follows:

1 = I did this **most of the time**   **2** = I did this **some of the time**   **3** = I **rarely** did this

My stance was:
clear – e.g. I changed the written language in the source to my own spoken language.   1 ☐ 2 ☐ 3 ☐
concise – e.g. I expressed one idea at a time.   1 ☐ 2 ☐ 3 ☐
critical – e.g. I acknowledged that academic ideas are complex, not black and white.   1 ☐ 2 ☐ 3 ☐

I interacted well by:
linking my ideas smoothly into the discussion – e.g. I linked my point to a point that had been mentioned before.   1 ☐ 2 ☐ 3 ☐
using active listening skills – e.g. I used eye contact, nodding, expressions of agreement.   1 ☐ 2 ☐ 3 ☐
not dominating – e.g. I allowed other students to break into the discussion.   1 ☐ 2 ☐ 3 ☐

My language was:
fluent – e.g. I was able to speak without a lot of hesitations.   1 ☐ 2 ☐ 3 ☐
accurate – e.g. I was able to use a range of grammar and vocabulary to express complex academic ideas.   1 ☐ 2 ☐ 3 ☐
clear – e.g. I used stress, intonation and pausing to express my meaning.   1 ☐ 2 ☐ 3 ☐

I cited:
from sources to support my stance – e.g. I didn't just rely on my own personal opinion in the discussion.   1 ☐ 2 ☐ 3 ☐
by mentioning the reliability of my source – e.g. I mentioned that the information I cited came from a reliable source (*The Journal of XX*/The World Health Organization).   1 ☐ 2 ☐ 3 ☐

This Unit's Focus
I paraphrased information without changing its meaning.   1 ☐ 2 ☐ 3 ☐
I transformed written language to spoken language naturally.   1 ☐ 2 ☐ 3 ☐

Ideas for future improvement

3
ETHICS

Expressing stance

Learning outcomes

By the end of this unit, you should be able to:

▸ identify features of a successful academic stance,

▸ write a stance which has an academic tone, is reasonable and well-justified,

▸ integrate counter-arguments and rebuttals into a stance to make it more critical,

▸ express agreement and disagreement with the stance of others in speaking, and

▸ use questions to make a tutorial discussion more critical and thoughtful.

ACADEMIC WRITING

Task 1

Express a personal opinion about an ethical issue

Imagine that you could go forward in time to before your future children (one male and one female) were born. At this time in the future, parents are able to select from a range of their own embryos for transplantation based on a "menu" of traits and abilities. However, they are able to choose only four traits for each child.

Look at the menu of traits below and answer the following questions:

1. Which four traits would you choose for your female child?

2. Which four traits would you choose for your male child?

3. Do you think it is ethically acceptable to use technology for embryo selection in this way? Why? Or why not?

"Mental" traits	Physical characteristics	"Athletic" traits	Personality traits
mathematical ability	hair colour	strong upper body	studiousness
musical ability	eye colour	strong lower body	dependability
ability to be empathetic	height	good balance	self-confidence
spirituality	weight	flexibility	sociability [e.g. ability to make friends]
ability to be loving	body type	good coordination	sensitivity
good memory	ability to age well	good endurance	independence

Mike and Jane are undergraduate students. They have two very different stances on the use of technology for embryo selection based on physical and mental traits.

"I think that embryo selection based on physical and mental traits is always a terrible idea!"

Mike

"I think that embryo selection based on physical and mental traits is always a great idea!"

Jane

These personal opinions are clear, but they are **not suitable** as an academic stance.

Task 2
Analyze the language of a successful academic stance

Look at the table below. Jane and Mike improve their personal opinions in four ways to make them more appropriate for an academic audience. Identify what these four changes are. Record the changes in the column on the left.

Change made	Mike	Jane	Stance is too personal/ emotional, not reasonable, not justified and not critical.
	I think that embryo selection based on physical and mental traits is always a terrible idea!	I think that embryo selection based on physical and mental traits is always a great idea!	
	~~I think that~~ Embryo selection based on physical and mental traits is always ~~a terrible idea!~~ ethically unacceptable.	~~I think that~~ Embryo selection based on physical and mental traits is always ~~a great idea!~~ ethically acceptable.	
	Embryo selection based on physical and mental traits is **mostly** ethically unacceptable.	Embryo selection based on physical and mental traits is, **on the whole**, ethically acceptable.	
	Embryo selection based on physical and mental traits is mostly ethically unacceptable **because it will lead to increased**	Embryo selection based on physical and mental traits is, on the whole, ethically acceptable **because parents have the moral**	

discrimination against
the poor who will not be
able to afford this type of
technology.

responsibility to give
their children the best
opportunities in life they
can afford.

Embryo selection based
on physical and mental
traits is mostly ethically
unacceptable because
it will lead to increased
discrimination against
the poor who will not be
able to afford this type of
technology. **Although it is
argued that this type of
technology will improve
the life of individual
children by giving them
more opportunities, the
effect on society as a
whole will be more social
inequality for people
too poor to afford the
technology and social
instability.**

Embryo selection based
on physical and mental
traits is, on the whole,
ethically acceptable because
parents have the moral
responsibility to give
their children the best
opportunities in life they
can afford. **Although it
has been claimed that this
will lead to discrimination
against people too poor
to afford the technology,
this is a reason to ensure
that the technology is
made accessible to as
many people as possible
through government
control. Discrimination
is not a reason to ban the
technology itself.**

Stance is
cautious,
well-justified,
critical
and has an
academic
tone (not
personal/
emotional).

Task 3
Identify and define a counter-argument and rebuttal

Look again at the final successful stance for Jane and Mike.

Identify which part of the stance is the counter-argument and which part is the rebuttal.
Underline the counter-argument and circle the rebuttal.

Now, define the two terms.

A counter-argument is ....

....

....

A rebuttal is ....

....

Features of a successful academic stance

The following table summarizes the features of a successful academic stance which you have just been analyzing:

A successful academic stance should be:	A successful academic stance should:
• written using an **academic tone**	‣ take out emotional adjectives/nouns/verbs and personal references such as "I think"
• **cautious**	‣ include hedging when appropriate
• **well-justified**	‣ include explanations and citations when appropriate
• **critical**	‣ include counter-arguments and rebuttals when appropriate

 ## Task 4
Identify stance in an academic essay

Read the essay below and decide whether it was written by Jane or Mike by identifying stance. Does the essay support (like Jane) or not support (like Mike) the use of technology for embryo selection? You will find the stance in multiple places in the essay. Also, underline the writer's stance in the essay.

ESSAY

Consider two cases. Michele and Michael have two embryos ready for implantation. Embryo A has XY sex chromosomes. Embryo B has XX. Should they be allowed to reject one embryo based on gender? Sex selection technology is currently being practised to varying degrees in many countries, although it is almost universally illegal. Consider the second case of Sally and Sam. Their embryo A has a gene that is linked to the propensity to be overweight, while B does not. Should they be allowed to reject embryo A? It is a possibility that tests in the future could identify a propensity (not 100% probability) to certain traits related to appearance, although this is not possible now. However, as we rush to gain a deeper understanding of the link between genetics and why some of us are more beautiful, more intelligent, etc., it is necessary to ask ourselves whether it is advisable to use pre/post-pregnancy technology for embryo/

fetus selection of non-disease traits. This essay argues that the use of such technology is unwise because it has the potential to cause greater harm than good for society as a whole, leading to an increase in social instability and inequality. The issues raised in the two cases above will be used to support this stance throughout the essay.

The main argument supporting the use of pre/post-pregnancy technology for non-disease states, such as gender and appearance, is that parents have the moral responsibility to "select" the best children that they could have based on the information available to them. One major proponent of this argument is Professor Savulescu, Uehiro Professor of Practical Ethics at the University of Oxford. He believes that "couples (or single reproducers) should select the child, of the possible children they could have, who is expected to have the best life, or at least as good a life as the others, based on the relevant, available information" (Savulescu, 2002, p. 415). He believes that technology should be used to give parents as much information as possible about their future child, that they should be given free choice which child to have, and "advice as to which child will be expected to enter life with the best opportunity of having the best life" (p. 425). Admittedly, making decisions which are in the best interests of others is, of course, a moral good. However, people have a greater moral responsibility to act according to the good of society as a whole. Humans exist and thrive within a social network, and if that social network is harmed, we are all, in turn, harmed. This means that moral decisions need to be made primarily at the social level for the good of all and this technology has been shown to lead to certain types of social instability.

The current use of sex selection technology is the prime example of the link between pre/post-pregnancy technology and social instability. The use of this technology in countries where there is a "combination of son preference, easy access to sex-selection technologies and abortion" (Hesketh & Jiang, 2012, p. 3) has led to unbalanced sex ratio at birth (SRB) rates. For example, in 2011, the SRB for China was reported to be 118 (National Bureau of Statistics of China, as cited in Hesketh & Jiang, 2012) – 118 males for every 100 females. Extensive use of ultrasound screening and selective abortion has led to approximately 30 million more males under the age of 20 than females (Zhu, Li & Hesketh, 2009). In India, one large-scale study reported that the SRB was 132 for second births when the first birth was a female and 139 for third births with two previous female births (Jha, Kumar, Vasa et al., 2006). While these skewed SRBs are also a result of better health care and food for boys, female infanticide and a high rate of death in childbirth (Allahbadia, 2002), it is clear from research that the use of sex selection technologies plays a significant role in the high male-to-female ratios (Jha, Kumar, Vasa et al., 2006; Zhu, Li & Hesketh, 2009).

The result of these unbalanced SRBs is that a significant proportion of men are unable to marry and this also leads to social instability. In the countries mentioned above, social status is strongly related to marital status. Men who are left unmarried are largely the poor and uneducated, further increasing social inequalities (Lichter, Anderson & Hayward, 1995). High SRBs have been linked to increases in prostitution, kidnapping and trafficking of women in China (Tucker, Henderson, Wang et al., 2005) and in other parts of Asia (Hudson & Den Boer, 2004). Hudson and Den Boer also attribute a recent large increase in dowry prices in parts of India to the shortage of women. All of the above can lead to social instability. While Savulescu might argue that the parents of these male children have ensured the "best life" for their child, this is not always true as many of these males are likely to suffer from low self-esteem if they can't fulfill societal expectations such as marriage and procreation. One recent study using in-depth interviews, for example, showed that older unmarried men in Guizhou province reported feeling depressed and hopeless because of their single status (Zhou, Wang, Li & Hesketh, 2011).

It is also important to look to the future and consider the ethical implications of developing pre/post-pregnancy technology. It is feasible that technology might develop in the future to allow screening for desirable attributes related to appearance. Ideals of beauty are social and cultural concepts. It has been shown that people who don't meet those ideals suffer discrimination. For example, Judge and Cable (2004) found from an analysis of 45 studies that height was significantly correlated with career success and that a person who is 72 inches tall is likely to earn $166,000 more over a career than someone who is 65 inches tall. Widespread discrimination has also been shown based on weight in multiple domains such as the workplace, education and health care (Puhl & Brownell, 2001). It might seem logical, therefore, that parents use such technology to ensure the "best life" for their children. In fact, if we look at the effect on society as a whole, as we did with sex selection, it seems that a widespread use of this technology would lead to even less tolerance for diversity than exists now and therefore greater social inequality for those without access to such technology for economic reasons. This would lead to greater discrimination. What this means is that while there might be benefits for individual children born from the use of this technology, on the societal level, the effect would be much greater social inequality.

Establishing an equitable and stable society is the responsibility of every individual who makes up that society. Establishing a society like this will sometimes require people to act against their own individual best interest for the sake of the greater good. The use of pre/post-pregnancy technology is an example of this. While selecting traits such as gender and appearance might lead to individuals having a "best life", the harm that this does to society as a whole outweighs the benefits to the individual. There needs to be regular and timely consultation about this issue between policy makers, ethicists, medical and legal professionals, and the general public.

References

Allahbadia, G. (2002). The 50 million missing women. *Journal of Assisted Reproductive Genetics*. 19(9):411–416.

Hesketh, T., & M. Jiang (2012). The effects of artificial gender imbalance. Science & Society Series on Sex and Science. *EMBO Report*. 13(6): 487–492.

Hudson, V., & A. Den Boer (2004). *Bare Branches: The Security Implications of Asia's Surplus Male Population*. Cambridge, MA: MIT Press.

Jha, P., R. Kumar, P. Vasa, N. Dhingra, D. Thiruchelvam, & R. Moineddin (2006.) Low female-to-male sex ratio of children born in India: national survey of 1.1 million households. *Lancet* 367: 211–218.

Judge, T. & D. Cable (2004). The effect of physical height on workplace success and income: Preliminary test of a theoretical model. *Journal of Applied Psychology*. 89 (3): 428–441.

(The remaining references have been taken out to save space.)

Critical argumentation: Using counter-arguments and rebuttals

As you saw in Task 2, integrating counter-arguments and rebuttals into your academic writing is important because it strengthens your stance. It also shows that you:

- understand the complexities of the topic,

- are less biased, and

- have good critical thinking skills.

Your argumentation becomes **logically stronger** and **more persuasive** through the use of counter-arguments and rebuttals.

A typical critical argument structure looks like this:

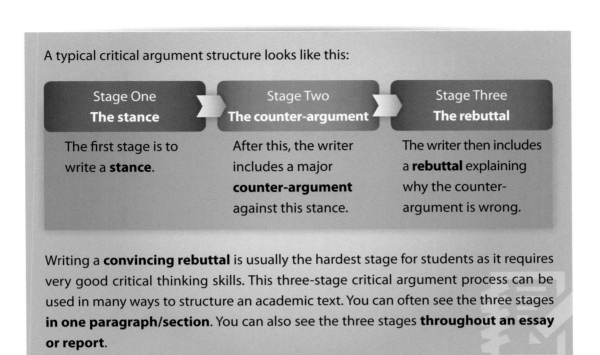

Stage One **The stance**	Stage Two **The counter-argument**	Stage Three **The rebuttal**
The first stage is to write a **stance**.	After this, the writer includes a major **counter-argument** against this stance.	The writer then includes a **rebuttal** explaining why the counter-argument is wrong.

Writing a **convincing rebuttal** is usually the hardest stage for students as it requires very good critical thinking skills. This three-stage critical argument process can be used in many ways to structure an academic text. You can often see the three stages **in one paragraph/section**. You can also see the three stages **throughout an essay or report**.

Task 5
Identify the differences between three possible critical argument structures

There are **many** ways that this critical argument structure could be used to organize an essay. The table below shows you three ways. Analyze the three examples and:

1. fill in the boxes which are empty, and

2. discuss how this structure compares with the structure of the essays you wrote at secondary school.

	Structure One	Structure Two	Structure Three
Introduction	Stance	Stance	Stance
Paragraph 1	1st argument supporting stance	1st argument supporting stance	Counter-argument for stance + Rebuttal
Paragraph 2	2nd argument supporting stance	Counter-argument for 1 + Rebuttal	1st argument supporting stance + Counter-argument for 1 + Rebuttal

		2nd argument supporting stance	
Paragraph 3			
Paragraph 4	Counter-argument for 1, 2 and 3 + Rebuttal		3rd argument supporting stance + Counter-argument for 3 + Rebuttal
Conclusion	Summary of stance and arguments 1, 2 and 3	Summary of stance and arguments 1 and 2	Summary of stance and arguments 1, 2 and 3

Task 6

Identify critical argument structure in an academic text

Read the essay again. Does the argument structure in the essay match Structure One, Two or Three from the table above?

The argument structure in the essay matches Structure _____ from the table above.

You have already underlined the stance in the essay. Now identify the rest of the critical argument structure in the essay by highlighting the following in different colours:

1. the counter-arguments

2. the rebuttals

Label each of these in the right column of the essay on pages 65–68.

The introduction has been done for you below:

ESSAY	Argument structure
Consider two cases. Michele and Michael have two embryos ready for implantation. Embryo A has XY sex chromosomes. Embryo B has XX. Should they be allowed to reject one embryo based on gender? Sex selection technology is currently being practised to varying degrees in many countries, although it is almost universally illegal. Consider the second case of Sally and Sam. Their embryo A has a gene that is linked to the propensity to be overweight, while B does not. Should they be allowed to reject embryo A? It is a possibility that tests in the future could identify a propensity (not 100% probability) to certain traits related to appearance, although this is not possible now. However, as we rush to gain a deeper understanding of the link between genetics and why some of us are more beautiful, more intelligent, etc., it is necessary to ask ourselves whether it is advisable to use pre/post-pregnancy technology for embryo/fetus selection of non-disease traits. **This essay argues that the use of**	← Stance
such technology is unwise because it has the potential to cause greater harm than good for society as a whole, leading to an increase in social instability and inequality. The issues raised in the two cases above will be used to support this stance throughout the essay.	

Task 7
Practise expressing stance and using critical thinking skills

You are going to practise writing counter-arguments and rebuttals on six issues related to science, technology and ethics. To prepare for this, debate the six topics in groups of three. Debating will give you ideas for your writing.

Get into groups of three. Debate the six issues by playing one of the following roles:

- Student 1 argues **for** the stance.
- Student 2 argues **against** the stance.
- Student 3 **judges** whether Student 1 or 2 has the most convincing arguments.

You will have **2 minutes** for each debate and the judge will have **30 seconds** to say who had the most convincing arguments and **why**.

Switch roles every time you debate a new issue. You will have two chances to play each role.

Stance 1
The use of live animals in scientific experiments is justifiable.

Stance 2
Euthanasia should be legal for terminally ill patients.

Stance 3
Genetically modified crops are necessary.

Stance 4
Nuclear energy should be the primary form of energy used by governments.

Stance 5
Factory farming (raising livestock such as chickens in confined spaces) should be banned.

Stance 6
Governments' use of surveillance should be strictly regulated and they should be required to notify people when they are being watched.

Task 8
Identify language used to signal the counter-argument and the rebuttal

Look at the words/phrases listed below. Some of these words/phrases are used in writing to **signal the counter-argument** to the reader and some are used to **signal the rebuttal**.

Admittedly,	Opponents/critics of this position believe that . . .	
While it is true that . . .	Nevertheless, . . .	In fact . . .
This claim is not justified because . . .		It might seem that . . .
This is not true because . . .		

Put them in the right place in the table on page 73 and add two more examples of your own for each column. Some of the words/phrases might fit in both columns.

Language used to signal the counter-argument	Language used to signal the rebuttal
• • • • My examples:	• • • • My examples:

Task 9
Practise writing counter-arguments and rebuttals

Now you should be ready to practise writing counter-arguments and rebuttals. Use the supporting and opposing arguments you and your group members used in the debates in Task 7 to write a critical stance for four of the issues you debated. You should do this by:

1. **adding a justification** for the stance,

2. **adding a counter-argument** against that stance,

3. **adding a rebuttal** which explains why the counter-argument is wrong,

4. indicating where you would need to **include a citation** to back up your stance, and

5. using some of the language from the table above to **signal** the counter-argument and the rebuttal.

The first stance has been done for you as an example.

Issue 1: Genetically modified crops are necessary *because the rising population requires the production of pest resistant crops with a high yield* [citation]. *Even though many opponents of genetic modification (GM) have claimed that these crops are a risk to our health* [citation], *there have been no reliable unbiased studies that have shown that the GM itself, rather than the pesticides that are sometimes used alongside the GM food, are harmful* [citation]. *GM food is so widespread now* [citation] *that if it were harmful to health, there would be evidence to prove it.*

Issue 2: Nuclear energy should be the primary form of energy used by governments
because . . .

Issue 3: Factory farming (raising livestock such as chickens in confined spaces) is necessary in today's world *because . . .*

Task 10
Assess your partner's counter-arguments and rebuttals

Swap your work with your partner. Ask him or her to assess your writing using the criteria below:

	Peer assessment of Issue 2		Peer assessment of Issue 3	
You have a **clear and logical justification** for your stance.	Yes	No	Yes	No
You have a **clear and logical counter-argument** against the stance.	Yes	No	Yes	No
You have a **clear and logical rebuttal** which explains why the counter-argument is wrong.	Yes	No	Yes	No
You have correctly **indicated where the citations are needed**.	Yes	No	Yes	No
You have used **signalling language correctly** to show where the counter-argument and the rebuttal are.	Yes	No	Yes	No

Hedging: The importance of being cautious

When you express a stance, you need to think about how strong you want to make that stance. You need to think about whether you can claim that something is:

definitely true	true **all the time**	true for **all people**	true in **all contexts**
probably true	true only for **some of the time**	true only for **some people**	true only in **some contexts**

It is important that you are **cautious** when expressing stance. If you over-generalize, you run the risk of being criticized by the person assessing your writing.

Task 11
List hedging words

The following table has three different categories of hedging words commonly used in academic writing. Add five examples to each category. Put them in order of strength.

Frequency	Certainty	Quantity	
all the time	definitely	all	**Strong**
....	....	....	
....	....	....	
....	....	....	
....	....	....	
....	....	....	
infrequently	possibly	a small proportion	**weak**

Task 12
Improve a paragraph

The following paragraph has two problems:

1. The tone is too personal/emotional.

2. Some of the statements are not cautious enough. They need to be hedged.

Identify the words in the text that need changing. Correct the text.

1   I think it is really cruel to use live animals in experimental testing. It should be allowed

2   because of the benefits it brings to human health. This kind of testing has led to

3   amazing improvements in medical treatments for cancer (Hausen et al. 2002) and

4   HIV (Rickman et al. 2009). It has led to the development of vaccines (Morgan et al.

5   2000) and medical treatments such as insulin (Nagano et al. 2005). It has also allowed

6   scientists to determine the safe level of exposure to common chemicals (Vanderberg

7   2010). Some opponents claim that these benefits are outweighed by the suffering

8   which animals endure and that other types of testing should be used instead, such

9   as the use of cell cultures. This technique should be used when possible, however, its

10   use is limited. Tests using cell cultures can only show effects on the molecular level

11   (Burns 2005) whereas animal testing can show systematic effects around the body.

12   Legislative regulations have been put in place in countries to stop animals being

13   tortured in experimental research (Baumans 2004). These regulations are largely based

14   on the three "Rs" first described by Russell and Burch (1959) – Replacement, Reduction,

15   Refinement. For example, 1. animal tests should be replaced by other techniques,

16   when possible, 2. the number of animal used should be reduced when possible and 3.

17   experimental techniques used should be refined to stop the agony and misery that the

18   poor animals feel.

Task 13
Express stance in your own paragraph

Now, let's put everything you have learnt in this unit so far together.

Remember what you have learnt about writing a successful academic stance on page 65. A successful academic stance should:

- be written using an **academic tone** (not emotional or personal),
- be **cautious** (include hedging where necessary),
- be **well-justified** (include explanations and citations), and
- be **critical** (include counter-arguments and rebuttals).

Write your own paragraph based on the stance that *euthanasia should be legal for terminally ill patients*. Use the notes on page 78 to help you.

Euthanasia for terminally ill patients

- Aim = ↓ mental and physical suffering
- Doctors' ethical principle = act in the best interests of the patient (Herring, 2012)
- Not many beds in palliative care hospices (Zerzan et al., 2000)
- Wide-spread research = hospices don't give enough pain relief/counselling (Jennings et al., 2011)
- Terminal illness → lots of pain + depression (Natan, 2010)

Homework

Prepare for a tutorial discussion

Get together with your tutorial discussion group members and choose one of the following issues for your next tutorial discussion:

Issue 1	**Issue 2**	**Issue 3**
The use of live animals in scientific experiments	Euthanasia for terminally ill patients	Genetically modified crops

Issue 4	**Issue 5**	**Issue 6**
Nuclear energy	Factory farming (raising livestock such as chickens in confined spaces)	Governments' use of surveillance

To prepare, search for information on Google Scholar and your library's electronic databases for at least three sources on this issue. Read the texts and take notes. Include the references for your source texts.

ACADEMIC SPEAKING

Making your academic discussions more critical

Academic discussions are usually based around issues which are debatable. Such discussions require you to form a personal stance based on your knowledge and reading.

During the discussion, it is likely that there will be at least one time when you disagree with someone's stance. You should see this moment as an opportunity to **deepen** the discussion and make it more **critical** by **challenging the stance**. It is through disagreement that **deeper learning** happens. This **deep learning** is **highly valued** at university.

There are many types of challenges that you will likely make in a discussion. The two main types of challenges are:

- challenging the stance, and
- challenging the source that the stance is based on.

Some examples are listed in the table below:

Challenging the stance	Challenging the source
1. Stance is **wrong**.	1. Source is **too old**.
2. Stance is **over-generalized**.	2. Source is **biased/not reliable**.
3. Stance **appeals to emotion rather than logic**.	3. **Ideas/statistics** in source **don't support the stance** (may be in wrong context/wrong time frame).
4. Stance **contains a cause/effect relationship which is wrong** (might be correlation instead).	4. Evidence for stance is given but source is **missing**.

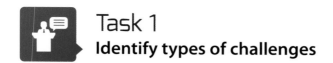

Task 1
Identify types of challenges

Below are a series of stances on the topic of genetically modified (GM) crops. Write the most appropriate type of challenge in the right column using the list on page 80.

Two examples have been given. There is more than one possible answer for some stances.

Challenging the stance	What type of challenge could you use?
"People want GM food labelled."	
"GM crops cause cancer. Rates of cancer have risen at the same time as the number of GM crops has risen."	
"All GM crops are unsafe."	*Stance is wrong.*
"We have to have GM crops, otherwise poor people will starve."	

Challenging the source	What type of challenge could you use?
"GM crops are more profitable for farmers. Even though GM seeds cost more, the overall cost from seed purchase to harvest is lower than conventional crops. An article from the *Journal of Trends in Plant Science* stated that GM seeds are, on average, 20% more expensive."	
"Risk analysis shows that the benefits of GM crops far outweigh the negatives. This is confirmed by a 1996 study from the *Journal of Nature Biotechnology* which analyzed the case studies of 20 different GM crops."	
"Too much agricultural land is made up of GM crops. The percentage in the US is 16.5%."	*Evidence for stance is given but source is missing.*
"GM crops have the same environmental impact as non-GM crops. For example, a report by Monsanto* shows that Roundup Ready corn has no worse impact than conventional corn."	

*Monsanto is one of the largest companies producing genetically engineered seeds.

The language of polite challenges

You might feel shy about challenging each other's ideas. Remember, challenging each other will lead to a more critical discussion and, in turn, deeper learning on your part. It will also provide your peers an opportunity to defend their stance.

So, how can you challenge in a way that is polite and non-threatening?

The first way is to **use hedging to soften the challenge**.
Instead of saying *"That's not true because ..."*, you can say:

- *I don't think that's true because ...*

- *That might/may not be true because ...*

- *That's probably not true because ...*

- *I wonder if that is true because ...*

The second way is to **change the challenge from a statement into a question**.
A question is less threatening than a statement. It also requires an answer and this helps to keep the conversation moving.

- *Have you thought about ... ?*

- *What do you think about ... ?*

- *What about ... ?*

- *Are you sure ... ?*

- *Is it possible ... ?*

- *Is it likely that ... ?*

Challenging is important, but it should not be done **all the time**. If you challenge very frequently, the discussion will become dysfunctional. Also, challenging the stance of others should not be the only thing that you contribute to a discussion. You need to have a good balance between challenging the stance of others and adding your own stance to the discussion.

Task 2
Identify polite challenges

Look again at each of the stances. Write a challenging statement and a challenging question for each which is polite and non-threatening. Make sure your challenging statement/question focuses on the type of challenge you identified in Task 1 on page 81. Two examples have been given below.

Challenging the stance	Example of challenging statement	Example of challenging question
"People want GM food labelled." **[stance is over-generalized]**		
"GM crops cause cancer. Rates of cancer have risen at the same time as the number of GM crops has risen." **[cause/effect relationship is wrong]**		
"All GM crops are unsafe." **[stance is incorrect]**	I **don't think** that this is possible. If it were true, a large percentage of the population would be sick.	Are you sure that is right?
"We have to have GM crops, otherwise poor people will starve." **[stance is based on emotion rather than logic]**		

Task 3
Practise critical questioning

Get into groups of three. Debate three issues you discussed previously.

Issue 1	Issue 2	Issue 3
The use of live animals in scientific experiments	Euthanasia for terminally ill patients	Genetically modified crops

For each issue, take on one of the following roles:

- Student 1: <u>express your stance</u> on the topic.

- Student 2: <u>ask challenging questions about the stance</u>.

- Student 3: <u>give feedback</u> on the **logic of the challenging questions** and **whether the challenging questions were polite**.

Switch roles every time you debate a new issue.

You will have **two minutes** for each debate and the judge will have **one minute** to give feedback.

The flowchart below shows how to structure your debate:

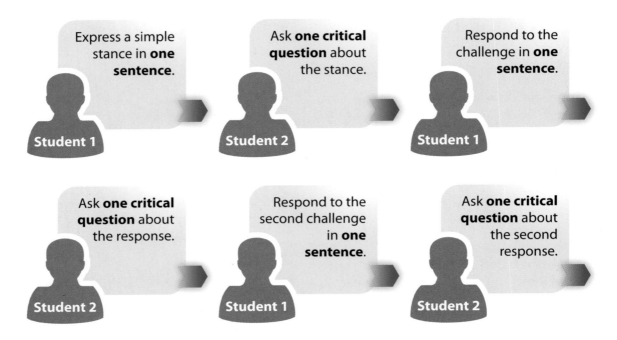

Student 2 should only ask challenging questions about the stance, not about sources, as Student 1 will not have any sources.

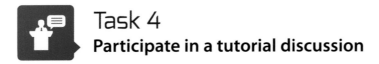

Task 4
Participate in a tutorial discussion

Now, hold a 30-minute tutorial discussion with your group members on the topic that you chose on page 79.

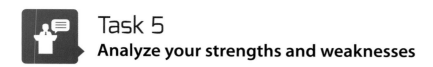

Task 5
Analyze your strengths and weaknesses

Take five minutes to fill in the form below. Rate your overall performance on each criterion as follows:

1 = I did this **most of the time**   **2** = I did this **some of the time**   **3** = I **rarely** did this

My stance was: **clear** – e.g. I changed the written language in the source to my own spoken language. **concise** – e.g. I expressed one idea at a time. **critical** – e.g. I acknowledged that academic ideas are complex, not black and white.	1 ☐ 2 ☐ 3 ☐ 1 ☐ 2 ☐ 3 ☐ 1 ☐ 2 ☐ 3 ☐
I interacted well by: **linking my ideas smoothly into the discussion** – e.g. I linked my point to a point that had been mentioned before. **using active listening skills** – e.g. I used eye contact, nodding, expressions of agreement. **not dominating** – e.g. I allowed other students to break into the discussion.	1 ☐ 2 ☐ 3 ☐ 1 ☐ 2 ☐ 3 ☐ 1 ☐ 2 ☐ 3 ☐
My language was: **fluent** – e.g. I was able to speak without a lot of hesitations. **accurate** – e.g. I was able to use a range of grammar and vocabulary to express complex academic ideas. **clear** – e.g. I used stress, intonation and pausing to express my meaning.	1 ☐ 2 ☐ 3 ☐ 1 ☐ 2 ☐ 3 ☐ 1 ☐ 2 ☐ 3 ☐
I cited: **from sources to support my stance** – e.g. I didn't just rely on my own personal opinion in the discussion. **by mentioning the reliability of my source** – e.g. I mentioned that the information I cited came from a reliable source (*The Journal of XX*/The World Health Organization).	1 ☐ 2 ☐ 3 ☐ 1 ☐ 2 ☐ 3 ☐
This Unit's Focus I asked critical questions when necessary. I interacted politely and in a non-threatening way.	1 ☐ 2 ☐ 3 ☐ 1 ☐ 2 ☐ 3 ☐

Ideas for future improvement

4
CHINA and ASIA

Synthesizing ideas in a paragraph or section

Learning outcomes

By the end of this unit, you should be able to:

▸ logically connect ideas within a paragraph or a section,
▸ write accurate and appropriate section headings,
▸ connect ideas through the use of cohesive devices and strategies,
▸ synthesize ideas from multiple sources,
▸ link your speaking turn to what has been previously said, and
▸ change focus within an academic discussion.

ACADEMIC WRITING

Task 1
Prepare for a role-play discussion

Discuss the following question with a classmate and justify your reasoning:

> **Which is more important to focus on in your country,**
> **the *environment* or the *economy*?**

Task 2
Participate in a role-play discussion

Form a group of three with your classmates. Each student will choose one of the following roles:

Student 1

You are a representative from the Department of Labour in China. You are responsible for achieving high employment rates in China and believe that this should be top priority for the future of the country. Convince the top leader that the economy should be the focus for the future.

Student 2

You are a representative from the Department of Environmental Protection in China. You are responsible for the country's environmental beauty and protection and believe that this should be top priority for the future of the country. Convince the top leader that the environment should be the focus for the future.

Student 3

You are a top leader of the country listening to the representatives from the Department of Labour and the Department of Environmental Protection. You are responsible for both departments and the direction that China takes in allocating resources for the future. Moderate the discussion and decide who you agree with. Be sure to challenge their ideas and reasons.

In your groups, assume your roles and conduct the role-play discussion for 15 minutes.

 Task 3
Read for stance

The following report covers issues discussed in the role play that you just conducted on the economy and environment in China. Read the report and answer the following questions with a partner:

1. What is the writer's stance on the issue of the economy and environment in China?

2. Circle any supporting arguments that are similar to those that you heard or discussed in the role play.

3. Underline any supporting arguments that were not mentioned in the role play, but would have been useful.

Tough Choices Ahead: An Emphasis on Economic or Environmental Challenges?

1. Introduction

In a recent Global Risks Report (1),* environmental and economic issues were listed as top concerns that "will present unprecedented challenges to global and national resilience" (p. 17). As the world's most populous nation and its second largest economy, China not only manifests these issues, but, by its sheer size and pivotal role in an interconnected world, also imposes them onto the world. As a result, tough choices await China in balancing these two concerns. The aim of this report is to describe the current economic and environmental situation in China and, given the limited resources available, to evaluate which should receive immediate attention. This report will first review the slowing Chinese economy and China's worsening environment. It will then illustrate why attention needs to be shifted from economic issues to environmental concerns.

2. Challenges on Two Fronts: Economic and Environmental

This section discusses the challenges that China faces in its economy and environment.

2.1. Declining Economic Growth

Decelerating growth in China's GDP presents economic complications for multiple stakeholders. While China has seen unparalleled economic expansion in the past 30 years, many suspect that such expansion will not continue (2)(3). For instance, China's GDP most recently expanded by 7.7%, which was a decline from the previous period and markedly slower than expected (4). This slowdown can have negative implications for connected economies such as Taiwan, South Korea,

---

* Numbering reference system is used; the reference list can be found on page 91.

Brazil, Australia, and Germany as well as Africa, which counts China as its third largest trading partner (5). Apart from outside stakeholders, Chinese rural workers have already been negatively impacted by their country's weakening economy (6). These Chinese rural workers were more adversely affected by the decline in growth than any other social group due to higher unemployment (6). Possible consequences include further income inequality, social unrest, and additional strain on younger generations who often need jobs to carry the burden of providing for their parents.

2.2. Deterioration of the Environment

In addition to a stagnant economy, China also faces ongoing environmental issues. Among these include air pollution — a noticeably extreme problem — as China, according to Liu and Diamond (7), "has 16 of the world's 20 cities with the worst air pollution" (p. 37). A critical concern is that this statistic is likely to worsen. Coal, a major contributor to air pollution, accounted for approximately 70% of China's energy sources (8). Even with conservative assumptions in economic growth, Shealy and Dorian (8) estimated that China would still utilize over 6 billion tons of coal in 2025, which is three times that produced and used in 2005. Indicators measuring broader environmental factors also point to a deteriorating environment. Emerson et al. (9) report that China's environmental performance index in 2012 ranked 116 out of 132 countries analyzed and is trending downwards. Taken together, these statistics show a debilitating environmental situation.

3. Shifting Focus to Environmental Issues

In light of the above overview on economic and environmental issues confronting China, this section provides justification for shifting attention from the economy to the environment.

3.1. Historical Perspectives: A Strengthened and Reformed Economy

While the current economic risks mentioned in section 2.1 are concerning, they are partially alleviated when China's historical economic improvements are considered. For instance, China's rapid GDP growth of 10% over the past 30 years has boosted its economy to the second largest globally (10). Apart from significant GDP growth as an indicator of improvement, the World Bank (10) reports that between 1981 and 2008, 600 million people were lifted out of poverty, representing a 71% decrease in poverty. A closer examination also reveals a more sophisticated economy. An example of this is China's shift towards a service-based economy, which has helped to raise wages and household income (11). This can potentially ease some of the high unemployment worries also discussed in section 2.1. Lastly, a declining Chinese economy is unlikely to be detrimental as current conservative predictions of 6.6% in GDP growth would still leave China on target to be a high-income country and to surpass the US in economic size by 2030 (12). All this suggests that the current economic challenges mentioned in section 2.1, after accounting for the improvements made to a weak Chinese economy 30 years ago, are manageable and perhaps less of a concern.

3.2. Justifying Concentration on Environmental Challenges

In view of the relatively mild challenges on the economic front, a greater focus on the environment can be further justified in two ways. First, despite the severity of the situation, as discussed in section 2.2, existing policies designed to preserve the environment still show considerable deficiencies. Liu and Diamond (7) contend that "although more than 100 environmental laws and regulations exist in China, they are often ignored by local government leaders" (p. 37). A highly publicized example of the probable consequences of such weak enforcement is evident in the reporting of Beijing's poor air quality and visibility (14) (15) (16). Additionally, tax policies towards renewable energy projects have not been favourable; when compared with conventional energy projects, renewable energy projects often receive similar or higher taxation (13). However, the negative impacts of ignoring the environment are apparent not only in the environment, but also the Chinese economy. Statistics on tourism and GDP, two economic indicators, show that pollution in China has had damaging consequences (17) (18). The extent of the economic damage from worsening environmental conditions has also been measured. The World Bank (19) calculated that the total cost of outdoor air pollution and water pollution to China's economy was approximately USD100 billion or 5.8% of GDP per year. Assessing the above, it is clearer that government policies and regulations for the environment require immediate attention. Perhaps even more significant, the aforementioned evidence strongly suggests that a greater focus on the environment rather than the economy would help to improve both.

4. Conclusion

From this report, it can be seen that a declining Chinese economy and deteriorating environmental conditions present significant challenges for China. While a slowdown in economics is a valid worry, significant environmental conflicts have arisen and require immediate attention. Rationale for this has been presented by considering a more historical view of China's economic position, newfound environmental concerns from citizens, flaws in current frameworks to solve such concerns, and the economic consequences of a degraded environment. A logical recommendation for improving current solutions is to ensure enforcement from multiple levels of government. Additionally, a reallocation of resources from the economy to the environment should be enacted. This has broad implications since larger expenditures on the environment could help China tackle both challenges.

Reference List

1. World Economic Forum. (2013). Global risks 2013: An initiative of the risk response network. Retrieved from http://reports.weforum.org/global-risks-2013/
2. Haltmaier, J. (2013). Challenges for the future of Chinese economic growth (Paper Number 1072). Retrieved from Board of Governors of the Federal Reserve System, International Finance Discussion Papers website: http://www.federalreserve.gov/pubs/ifdp/2013/1072/ifdp1072.htm
3. Silk, R. (2013, 9 July). Economists see further slowdown in China. The Wall Street Journal. Retrieved from http://online.wsj.com/article/SB10001424127887323823004578593200107930868.html
4. China's economy: Speed isn't everything. (2013, 20 April). The Economist. http://www.economist.com/news/leaders/21576400-hidden-consolation-disappointing-chinese-growth-more-modern-economy-speed-isnt
5. Schiere, R. (2011). Impact of the financial and economic crisis on China's trade, aid and capital inflows to Africa (No. 11). Retrieved from Development Research Department, African Development Bank website: http://www.afdb.org/fileadmin/uploads/afdb/Documents/Financial-Information/Impact_china.pdf

(The remaining references have been taken out to save space.)

Task 4
Identify the writer's logic and argumentation

Outline the logical flow of arguments and evidence presented in section 3.2 of the report on pages 90–91. Some have already been done for you.

Stance

_____

Supporting argument #1

Government policies are insufficient.

Supporting argument #2

_____

Evidence given

1. _____

2. Beijing's poor air quality and visibility

3. _____

Evidence given

1. _____

2. _____

Refinement of stance in light of evidence

1. _____

2. Helping the environment can also help the economy.

Ensuring a logical flow of ideas

After you have collected information from your notes, you need to organize it in a logical manner. The following academic features of a report section can be used:

1. Section headings/topic sentences (Tasks 5–7)

2. Cohesive devices and strategies (Tasks 8–9)

3. Synthesizing ideas from multiple sources (Tasks 10–11)

Task 5
Identify the appropriate report section heading

Without looking at the whole report again and referring only to the section/paragraph below, identify the most appropriate report section heading from items 1 to 5. Justify your answer in the box below.

1. Importance of Economic Progress

2. Environment

3. Risks of Ignoring the Economy

4. Reasons for Shifting Focus to the Environment

5. The Economy Needs Our Help Now

I think . . . because . . .

3.2

In view of the relatively mild challenges on the economic front, a greater focus on the environment can be further justified in two ways. First, despite the severity of the situation, as discussed in section 2.2, existing policies designed to preserve the environment still show considerable deficiencies. Liu and Diamond (7) contend that "although more than 100 environmental laws and regulations exist in China, they are often ignored by local government leaders" (p. 37). A highly publicized example of the probable consequences of such weak enforcement is evident in the reporting of Beijing's poor air quality and visibility (14) (15) (16). Additionally, tax policies towards renewable energy projects have not been favourable; when compared with conventional energy projects, renewable energy projects often receive similar or higher taxation (13). However, the negative impacts of ignoring the environment are apparent not only in the environment, but also the Chinese economy. Statistics on tourism and GDP, two economic indicators, show that pollution in China has had damaging consequences (17) (18). The extent of the economic damage from worsening environmental conditions has also been measured. The World Bank (19) calculated that the total cost of outdoor air pollution and water pollution to China's economy was approximately USD100 billion or 5.8% of GDP per year. Assessing the above, it is clearer that government policies and regulations for the environment require immediate attention. Perhaps even more significant, the aforementioned evidence strongly suggests that a greater focus on the environment rather than the economy would help to improve both.

Showing stance through section headings and topic sentences

Section headings are features commonly found in reports. Section headings are similar to topic sentences in that they need to accurately reflect the information in the section. Here are a few general principles to be aware of:

1. The heading should indicate the stance of the section.

   While there may be times you need a neutral heading, most sections have a stance that should be reflected in the heading. This will also depend on the type of report being written.

2. Most report headings throughout this book are formed through noun phrases or gerunds. Here are a few examples:

   Historical Perspectives: Strengthened and Reformed Economy [*colon is used for longer noun phrase*]

   Deterioration of the Environment [*noun phrase – this could serve as a noun in a sentence*]

   Shifting Focus to Environmental Issues [*noun phrase that begins with a gerund*]

Topic sentences are similar to section headings in that they also indicate stance. While they are commonly found in essays, they can also appear in reports. Here are some functions of topic sentences:

1. Reflect or summarize what the paragraph/section is about.

2. Indicate the stance of the paragraph/section.

3. Provide a transition between paragraphs/sections through the use of cohesive devices and strategies, which will be discussed in Tasks 8–9.

Task 6
Write report section headings and identify topic sentences

The following sections/paragraphs are from the report on pages 89–91. Without turning back to look at the full report:

1. Underline the topic sentences in each section and identify the functions of those topic sentences. The three functions of a topic sentence keep listed here:

- Reflect or summarize what the paragraph/section is about.

- Indicate the stance of the paragraph/section.

- Provide a transition between paragraphs through the use of cohesive devices and strategies.

2. Write alternative section headings on the blanks. The overall heading for section 3 has been completed for you.

---

2. --

This section discusses the challenges that China faces in its economy and environment.

2.1. --

Decelerating growth in China's GDP presents economic complications for multiple stakeholders. While China has seen unparalleled economic expansion in the past 30 years, many suspect that such expansion will not continue (2) (3). For instance, China's GDP most recently expanded by 7.7%, which was a decline from the previous period and markedly slower than expected (4). This slowdown can have negative implications for connected economies such as Taiwan, South Korea, Brazil, Australia, and Germany as well as Africa, which counts China as its third largest trading partner (5). Apart from outside stakeholders, Chinese rural workers have already been negatively impacted by their country's weakening economy (6). They reported that these Chinese rural workers were more adversely affected by the decline in growth than any other social group due to higher unemployment. Possible consequences include further income inequality, social unrest, and additional strain on younger generations who often need jobs to carry the burden of providing for their parents.

2.2. --

In addition to a stagnant economy, China also faces ongoing environmental issues. Among these include air pollution — a noticeably extreme problem — as China, according to Liu and Diamond (7), "has 16 of the world's 20 cities with the worst air pollution" (p. 37). A critical concern is that this statistic is likely to worsen. Coal, a major contributor to air pollution, accounted for approximately 70% of China's energy sources (8). Even with conservative assumptions in economic growth, Shealy and Dorian (8) estimated that China would still utilize over 6 billion tons of coal in 2025, which is three times that produced and used in 2005. Indicators measuring broader environmental factors also point to a deteriorating environment. Emerson et al. (9) report that China's environmental performance index in 2012 ranked 116 out of 132 countries analyzed and is trending downwards. In aggregate, these statistics show a debilitating environmental situation.

3. Shifting Focus to Environmental Issues

In light of the above overview on economic and environmental issues confronting China, this section provides justification for shifting attention from the economy to the environment.

3.1. --

While the current economic risks mentioned in section 2.1 are concerning, they are partially alleviated when China's historical economic improvements are considered. For instance, China's rapid GDP growth of 10% over the past 30 years has boosted its economy to the second largest globally (10). Apart from significant GDP growth as an indicator of improvement, the World Bank (10) reports that between 1981 and 2008, 600 million people were lifted out of poverty, representing a 71% decrease in poverty. A closer examination also reveals a more sophisticated economy. An example of this is China's shift towards a service-based economy, which has helped to raise wages and household income (11). This can potentially ease some of the high unemployment worries also discussed in section 2.1. Lastly, a declining Chinese economy is unlikely to be detrimental as current conservative predictions of 6.6% in GDP growth would still leave China on target to be a high-income country and to surpass the US in economic size by 2030 (12). All this suggests that the current economic challenges mentioned in section 2.1, after accounting for the improvements made to a weak Chinese economy 30 years ago, are manageable and perhaps less of a concern.

Task 7
Analyze report section headings

Exchange your answers with a partner and complete the checklist below on whether the section headings:

☐ reflect or summarize what the paragraph/section is about

☐ indicate the stance of the paragraph/section

☐ are written in the form of a noun phrase

Inform your partner of any improvements that can be made.

Task 8
Identify cohesion within a section

Return to section 3.2 in Task 5 and circle the words or phrases that connect each sentence together.

Example:

In view of the relatively mild challenges on the economic front, a greater focus on the (environment) can be further justified in (two ways). (First,) despite the severity of the situation, as discussed in section 2.2, existing policies designed to preserve the (environment) still show considerable deficiencies.

Cohesive devices and strategies

One way of ensuring that a paragraph/section is logically constructed is through the use of cohesive devices and strategies. They can help to clarify the relationship between your arguments, supporting evidence, counter-arguments, and your interpretation of the sources. Three common ways of doing this are:

1. **Referencing** – words such as *this, that, these, those, it, its, he, his, she, her, they,* and *them* can be used to refer to other sentences. Here are some examples:

   China's economic rise has been prominent over the last 30 years. This can be attributed to **3 major factors**. The first of **these** is the rise in investment from foreign countries. **Chan** (2010) states that investment rose by more than 150% within the same period. **He** also compared *this figure* to other developing countries' foreign investment numbers and found that China had the largest increase.

2. **Lexical Repetition** – the usage of synonyms and similar vocabulary or phrases can build cohesion across sentences in a paragraph/section. Here are some examples:

   China's economic rise has been prominent over **the last 30 years**. This can be attributed to 3 major factors. The first of these is the rise in **investment** from foreign countries. Chan (2010) states that **investment** rose by more than 150% within **the same period**. He also compared *this figure* to other developing countries' **foreign investment** numbers and found that China had the largest increase.

* Notice that referencing and lexical repetition can be combined to create a stronger cohesive effect

e.g. Compare the following sentences with the sentences above.
He also compared *this figure* to other developing countries'...
He also compared *this* to other developing countries'...

3. **Linking Words and Phrases** – these are words and phrases that signal the relationship between ideas. Here are some common categories and examples:

Additive (signalling more to come): *in addition, additionally, apart from, furthermore, similarly*, etc.

Contrasting (signalling an opposing idea): *however, although, even though, while*, etc.

Causal (signalling cause): *therefore, consequently, as a result, due to*, etc.

Example (signalling the onset of an example): *for example, for instance, to illustrate*, etc.

Task 9
Categorize and identify cohesive devices and strategies

Place all of the connections that you circled in Task 8 into the following categories of cohesion. For the Referencing and Lexical Repetition categories, write what each circle is connected to. Two examples have been completed for you.

Are there any cohesive devices and strategies that you missed in Task 8? If so, also place them into the appropriate category of cohesion.

Referencing	Lexical repetition	Linking words and phrases
• two ways – first • environmental laws and regulations – they	• ignored by local government leaders – weak enforcement	• however

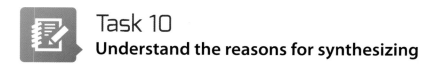

Task 10
Understand the reasons for synthesizing

There are two sentences with information cited from multiple sources in section 3.2 of the report. Why do you think the writer has done this? What relationship do the sources have with each other? Write your answer in the box below.

I think this is done because . . .

The relationship between the sources is . . .

Synthesizing information from your sources

When searching for evidence in your sources, you will find information that overlaps or differs. The process of combining this information for use in your writing is called synthesis. Here are a few examples of the ways that it can be done:

Example 1:
From Xu, 2011:
China has had major increases in economic output for the past 30 years.

From Chan, 2010:
For the last 30 years, China's economy has been outperforming expectations.

One possible synthesis:
China's economy has been strong for the past 30 years (Chan, 2010; Xu, 2011).

Example 2:
From Xu, 2011:
However, the environment has been essentially ignored with air pollution at record highs.

From Chan, 2010:
Statistics from the past 10 years show that air pollution has increased by more than 20%.

From Yin, 2011:
Regulations have helped to lower air pollution in some parts of China.

One possible synthesis:
While regulations in some areas of China have helped to decrease air pollution (Yin, 2011), statistics still indicate that air pollution has actually worsened in the past 10 years (Chan, 2010; Xu, 2011).

Here are some guidelines that the above synthesized examples followed:

1. Analyze the similarities and differences.

2. Use cohesive devices and strategies.

3. Accurately represent the meaning of the information being synthesized.

4. Synthesize by using one sentence or multiple sentences.

Task 11
Synthesize overlapping and contradictory information

The following information is from sources related to the economy and environment in China. Synthesize the information in Items 1–3 using all the sources. Complete Item 4 when you have finished.

(1)

From Smith, 2010:
Increasing concern for the environment has been met by intense opposition from corporations.

From Ellis, 2011:
Concern for the environment has been consistently opposed by corporations through promises of more jobs and higher paying salaries.

Your synthesis of the information from the two sources above:

(2)

From Lin, 2009:

While worries about the Chinese economy are valid, ignoring air pollution concerns will lead to further increases in dangerous pollutants such as nitrous and sulphur dioxide.

From Tompkins, 2010:

In China, the impact of job losses from shifting resources to the environment will not be viewed positively.

Your synthesis of the information from the two sources above:

(3)

From Chu, 2010:

Sulphur dioxide in air pollution in Southern China has increased by 25% in the past 5 years.

From Chan, 2009:

Recent figures show that Southern China has experienced significant increases in sulphur dioxide.

From Lu, 2013:

Recent measures of air pollutants such as sulphur dioxide have declined by 5% due to a slowdown in economic growth.

Your synthesis of the information from the two sources above:

(4) Analyze your synthesized sentence(s) by completing the checkboxes below:

- [ ] I have integrated information that overlapped and differed.

- [ ] I have used cohesive devices and strategies.

- [ ] My synthesis accurately represents the original meaning of the information from the sources.

- [ ] I have synthesized through one or multiple sentences.

Task 12
Prepare to write a paragraph/section

The last task of this writing section will require you to synthesize supporting arguments and counter-arguments in order to write a paragraph/section. Before you move onto this task, you will need to do the following:

1. Notice the box below containing information taken directly (word for word) from sources.

2. Notice the chart below the sources.

3. Read the stance in the chart on whether China should focus on the economy or the environment.

4. Categorize the information from the sources into the appropriate columns.

5. Think about how the supporting arguments can be used as rebuttals to the counter-arguments in order to support the given stance.

6. Look at the example provided in the chart for guidance.

From Fung, 2010, p. 120:
Statistics from the Department of Environmental Protection indicate that water and air pollution cost the Chinese economy approximately $6.5 billion USD in 2010. Much of this can be recovered by creating incentives for entrepreneurs to start companies and hire staff with the mission of reducing water and air pollution. Since 2001, companies servicing the environment have made profits of more than $10 billion USD in the United States and have employed over 300,000 people.

From Xu, 2011, p. 5:
With the aim of reducing air pollution, the government has already created numerous regulations to decrease the usage of coal in various parts of China.

From Li, 2012, p. 25:
Regulations aimed at controlling the use of coal have often gone ignored or given very little importance in many parts of China.

From Smith, 2013, p. 80:
While the economy has certainly cooled off from its peak in the mid-2000s, GDP, an indicator of economic power, is still growing at a steady pace of 8%, which is higher than most developing countries.

From Lan, 2013, p. 90:
In 2012, the levels of employment in China slowed to 8% growth from the previous year, its slowest growth rate in over 40 years.

From Xiao, 2013, p. 10:

What Chinese citizens need are jobs; while the environment is certainly an issue requiring solutions, draining resources used to create jobs in order to focus on the environment could lead to social instability from higher levels of unemployment.

Stance

Economic concerns still exist, but should focus on environment instead of economy; helping the environment can strengthen both the economy and the environment

Supporting arguments of this stance	Counter-arguments of this stance
1. From Smith, 2013: economy still growing at 8%, higher than most developing countries	1. From Lan, 2013: slowdown in growth to 8% is slowest in 40 years

I think . . .

Growth of 8% seems low if you only look at China, but looking at most developing countries, it's still high.

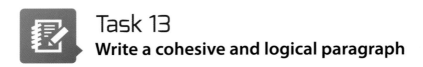

Task 13
Write a cohesive and logical paragraph

You will now write a paragraph/section of a report using the information from the sources that you just categorized. Use the stance given in the chart on page 103. You do not need to include all of the information from the sources. Remember to:

1. include a section heading,

2. write a topic sentence,

3. use cohesive devices and strategies to achieve cohesion,

4. paraphrase or quote when necessary, and

5. synthesize when necessary.

(Write your section heading here)

Task 14
Identify academic features in a paragraph/section

Exchange your paragraph/section with a classmate and then analyze his/her paragraph/section by answering the following questions:

1. Does the section heading summarize what the paragraph/section is about?	Yes	No
2. Is the section heading written in a noun phrase?	Yes	No
3. Does the section heading and topic sentence indicate the stance?	Yes	No
4. Are there examples of cohesive devices and strategies?	Yes	No
5. Are sources being synthesized appropriately?	Yes	No

Afterwards, compare the paragraph/section with the one in the answer key.

Homework
Prepare for a tutorial discussion

The issue of choosing more economic growth or solving environmental concerns is a global concern that can also be narrowed into specific issues. Hence, the next speaking tutorial topic will be chosen from a range of related topics. Form groups of five and choose one of the following topics. Conduct some research, formulate a stance, and take notes on your group's chosen topic:

1. Can renewable sources of energy help both the economy and the environment in China?

2. What should China do to help reverse global warming?

3. Should Southeast Asian countries focus on economic growth or environmental protection? What can be done to address both concerns?

4. Who should bear the most responsibility for global warming, developed or developing countries?

ACADEMIC
SPEAKING

Task 1
Link appropriately to what others have said

Below are three transcripts of spoken turns on the topic of economic concerns vs. environmental concerns in Southeast Asia. Discuss with a partner whether you think Transcript B or Transcript C does a better job of linking to Transcript A. Justify your answer.

Afterwards, discuss how you would improve the poorly linked transcript so that it appropriately links to Transcript A.

Transcript A

Today, we're going to discuss the issue of whether Southeast Asian countries should continue to focus on the economy or shift emphasis to the environment. Actually, I think that the environment should really be focused on more because the situation is getting worse. For example, according to an article in the *Journal of Pollution* written in 2010, air pollution has increased by 20% in the past 15 years. I think figures like this show examples of worsening environmental conditions that need attention.

Transcript B in response to the content in Transcript A

Yeah, I agree with you. Many of the Southeast Asian countries are very economically focused and you can see that in the lower tax rates that the governments give foreign and international corporations. These lower tax rates invite more companies to invest in those Southeast Asian countries and this means more jobs for their citizens. So it seems that economics is the most important concern for Southeast Asian countries.

Yeah, I think what you're saying about the worsening conditions in Southeast Asia is true. But, it seems that the environment is not their main concern right now. I think we need to remember that many of these Southeast Asian countries are still developing, and according to a report by Professor Ng in 2010, they have very small economies. This means that Southeast Asian citizens can probably see their worsening environmental conditions, but they realize that they also need jobs to continue to maintain their standard of living.

Linking your speaking turns and changing topics

In academic discussions, you need to link your arguments to what has been previously stated in the discussion. There are some set phrases and words to help you do this, but you also need to make your content relevant. As you saw in the transcripts above, using agreement language does not necessarily mean that your argument links logically with what was said before. Here are some guiding principles and language that you can use to improve the links in your spoken arguments:

1. Agree or disagree:

- I see your point, but . . .
- I also agree with that . . .
- I'm afraid I disagree with . . .
- Yes, I also agree with you on that.
- Yeah, but . . .

- That's right, I also . . .
- But, are you sure that . . . ?
- Hmm, I'm not sure about that because . . .
- I think that's a good point, but . . .
- Yeah, I also have evidence supporting your argument.

2. Reiterate what was just said in order to respond to an earlier point:

You may sometimes want to respond to an idea that was expressed by a student earlier in the discussion, but you also want to remain polite to the student who has just spoken. A good strategy for this is to first respond to the student who has just spoken through reiteration and then respond to the earlier point.

- Yeah, I completely agree with you, John, on . . . , but I'd also like to respond to Mike's idea of . . .

- (In response to John first) I think that's a good point about . . . , but to your argument Mike about . . .

3. Make your content relevant:

State your stance or evidence and show how it links with previously stated ideas and arguments.

4. Use appropriate language to change topics or perspectives:

There may be times when the discussion remains on a topic or perspective for too long and you feel it is appropriate to advance to another topic or perspective. Here are some examples of how you can do this:

- Well, it looks like we've figured out the . . . , I think it might be helpful to also talk about . . .

- So far, we've been talking about . . . , should we also focus on . . . ?

- That's a good point regarding . . . , but we should also think about . . .

The first part of each of these examples links backwards and the second part points to a new perspective.

Task 2
Prepare notes for a short discussion

You will soon discuss whether China should focus on the environment or economy with similar information that you used to write your section in Task 12 in the academic writing section. To prepare notes:

1. Notice the fourteen textboxes below and on the next page containing information from sources on the environment and economy.

2. Copy the information in the textboxes into the correct categories in the table on page 109. The first one has been completed for you as an example.

2012 – Water and air pollution cost economy $6.5 billion USD	2012 – employment slowed to 8% growth – slowest growth in jobs in 40 years
43% care more about economy rather than environment – still large percentage	Pollution clean-up companies in US made $10 billion in profit and created 300,000 jobs
Many regulations already exist to decrease use of coal in various parts of China	Air pollution → angry citizens → social instability

Taking resources away from economy → fewer jobs → unhappy citizens → social instability

Many health cases – patients had pre-existing health problems – may not be due to air pollution

Financial incentives can be given to entrepreneurs to open businesses to clean and prevent pollution

Laws aimed at limiting use of coal – often gone ignored in many parts of China

Cardiovascular (heart) problems from air pollution

Economy weakened considerably in 2012

2012 – Economy still growing at a steady pace of 7%, which is higher than most developed countries

Air pollution has devastating effects on health; e.g. asthma and lung cancer

Information that supports the stance of helping the environment	Information that supports the stance of helping the economy
Relates to economic impact	**Relates to economic impact**
1. 2012 – Water and air pollution cost economy $6.5 billion USD	1. Economy weakened considerably in 2012
2.	2.
3.	3.
4.	
Relates to legal issues	**Relates to legal issues**
1.	1.
Relates to health issues	**Relates to health issues**
1.	1.
2.	
Relates to social instability	**Relates to social instability**
1.	1.

Task 3
Practise linking and changing topics

Notice from your notes on the previous page that you have several perspectives (legal and health issues, social instability, economic impact) to use in order to support your own stance and agree with others. You also have possible areas for disagreement. To complete this task, here are the guidelines.

1. Form a group of four to discuss whether China should focus on the economy or the environment, using the notes you categorized on the previous page.

2. Two students should support the economy and the other two students should support the environment.

3. Notice the five categories of linking and changing topics below.

4. Check off a box when you are able to successfully perform a category.

5. Discuss for five minutes and then switch stances (i.e. switch to environment or economy) with your group members for more practice.

6. Try to check off at least one box in each category by practising each category during the discussions.

Link to **previous** point – AGREE ☐ ☐ ☐ ☐ ☐	Link to **previous** point – DISAGREE ☐ ☐ ☐ ☐ ☐
Link to **earlier** point – AGREE ☐ ☐ ☐ ☐ ☐	Link to **earlier** point – DISAGREE ☐ ☐ ☐ ☐ ☐

Change perspectives
☐ ☐ ☐ ☐ ☐

Task 4
Participate in a tutorial discussion

Now, hold a 30-minute tutorial discussion with your group members on the topic that you chose on page 105.

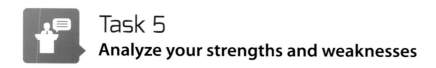

Task 5
Analyze your strengths and weaknesses

Take five minutes to fill in the form below. Rate your overall performance on each criterion as follows:

1 = I did this **most of the time**   **2** = I did this **some of the time**   **3** = I **rarely** did this

	1	2	3
My stance was:			
clear – e.g. I changed the written language in the source to my own spoken language.	☐	☐	☐
concise – e.g. I expressed one idea at a time.	☐	☐	☐
critical – e.g. I acknowledged that academic ideas are complex, not black and white.	☐	☐	☐
I interacted well by:			
linking my ideas smoothly into the discussion – e.g. I linked my point to a point that had been mentioned before.	☐	☐	☐
using active listening skills – e.g. I used eye contact, nodding, expressions of agreement.	☐	☐	☐
not dominating – e.g. I allowed other students to break into the discussion.	☐	☐	☐
My language was:			
fluent – e.g. I was able to speak without a lot of hesitations.	☐	☐	☐
accurate – e.g. I was able to use a range of grammar and vocabulary to express complex academic ideas.	☐	☐	☐
clear – e.g. I used stress, intonation and pausing to express my meaning.	☐	☐	☐
I cited:			
from sources to support my stance – e.g. I didn't just rely on my own personal opinion in the discussion.	☐	☐	☐
by mentioning the reliability of my source – e.g. I mentioned that the information I cited came from a reliable source (*The Journal of XX*/The World Health Organization).	☐	☐	☐
This Unit's Focus			
I linked the ideas in my turn with the ideas mentioned in previous turns.	☐	☐	☐
I used appropriate language to change topics.	☐	☐	☐

Ideas for future improvement

5
VALUES

Structuring a complete academic text

Learning outcomes

By the end of this unit, you should be able to:

- apply a range of structural features to help you organize an academic text clearly,
  - recognize the similarities and differences in report and essay structures,
    - create connections within your writing that direct the reader backwards and forwards, and
      - articulate strategies to ensure you continue to improve your discussion skills in the future.

ACADEMIC WRITING

 ## Task 1
Compare opinions about reality TV

Reality TV has become extremely popular over the last ten years. Before reading two texts on the topic, find out about other students' views on the topic. Follow the steps:

Step 1. Choose one question from the boxes below and write it on a piece of paper. Find a partner and ask each other your questions. Exchange opinions and give an example from your experience to support your stance.

Step 2. After two minutes, exchange question papers with your partner so that you have a different question. Find another student and ask each other your questions. Continue doing this until you have shared opinions with four students.

Step 3. After the activity, tell the class about the most interesting response you heard.

1. Do you enjoy watching reality TV? Why / Why not?	2. Why do you think reality TV has become so popular worldwide?	3. Is reality TV more beneficial or problematic to society?
4. Can reality TV be considered in any way educational?	5. Do you think children should watch reality TV?	6. What do you think motivates people to appear on reality TV?

Structuring academic texts

Academic texts are characterized by a clear structure which is represented in a number of ways, e.g. with *headings*, *subheadings*, *a numbering system*, *topic sentences* and *connections* drawn between *sentences* and *paragraphs/sections*. If a writer does not structure a text clearly, or as expected, it can be difficult to follow; it might be perceived as lacking in coherence.

The structure depends on the nature of the text, who it is for and what the context is. Some texts have a more obvious structure than others. For example:

- **A report** usually has headings, a numbering system, and even a table of contents if it is a long report. These help to guide the reader through the text.

- **An essay** has an introduction which tells the reader the focus and often the structure of the essay. It also has topic sentences to help guide the reader through the text. A journal article has an abstract and headings.

- **Non-academic texts** can also have a structure. A newspaper article, for example, begins with a headline and lead sentence to inform the reader of its content at a glance.

Preparing to read

In this unit you will work with two texts about reality TV on pages 116–122. Half of you will focus on the essay and the other half the report. You will then share your findings about structural features of the texts. First, form groups of four and decide who will read which text; two students should read the essay, and the other two the report.

Task 2
Identify the stance

Step 1. Skim through your text to identify the **overall stance** and **two main arguments**. If you are reading the essay, focus on the introduction, topic sentences and conclusion; if you are reading the report, focus on the introduction, headings and conclusion. Record them in the table on page 116 with your partner who has read the same text.

Step 2. When you have finished, compare your findings with the two students who read the other text and complete the final statement comparing the stances of the two pieces. Which arguments do you recognize from your initial discussions in Task 1?

Complete the table with the *stance* and *main arguments* from your text:

Essay	Report
Overall stance: Main arguments: 1. 2.	Overall stance: Main arguments: 1. 2.

The two texts have a similar stance as they are both .... ,

however, whilst the essay focuses on .... ,

the report focuses on ....

ESSAY

As a form of entertainment, reality TV has experienced a phenomenal growth in popularity over the last years, but do you think it does more harm than good to society?

The recent phenomenon of reality TV, although hugely popular worldwide, has at the same time met with considerable audience disapproval (Poniewozik et al., 2003). Its influence can be seen in outstanding ratings, for instance the 2012 final of *Britain's Got Talent* attracted an audience of nearly 14.5 million ("*Britain's Got Talent*", 2012) and the Nielsen Poll of Top US Prime Time Television 2012 placed seven reality shows in its top twenty.[1] Whilst such impressive audience figures indicate that reality TV could function as a valuable educational medium and promoter of civic values, this is not the priority of most money-making broadcasting networks whose main aim is to entertain. This essay will first discuss various moral issues of the genre, then move to consider how educational and social benefits generally come second to the demands of cheap entertainment, sometimes at the cost of individuals.

The main argument against reality TV is a moral one. Reality shows are often described as "humiliating" ("Is Reality TV Too Cruel?" 2012) and "deceptive" (Papacharissi & Mendelson, 2007).

---

[1] US Survey: Nielsen Tops of 2012: Television. Data from 1 January 2012. English and Spanish-language telecasts on Broadcast and Cable, Total Day.

The weaknesses and misfortunes of participants are revealed as audiences enjoy a display of hopefuls who can't sing, cooks who can't cook, and other failures. As Poniewozik (2003) indicates, what is remarkable about this "discomfort TV" is the ability of participants to rise above their insufficiencies. But this is the thing that Poniewozik believes audiences find so appealing; the message appears to be that in the pursuit of dreams, embarrassment can and will occur, but we actually have the power to rise above failure and live to fight another day relatively unharmed. Whilst the humiliation of candidates who choose to appear on a game show where the "rules" are known is quite possibly acceptable, it becomes questionable when contestants are openly deceived, as in *Joe Millionaire*, where women compete for the favours of a construction worker pretending to be a millionaire.

Humiliation and deception are definitely a concern, but more worrying is the effort some shows go to in search of new and often dangerous ways to maintain audience ratings. In some extreme competitions, participants take part in dangerous challenges for which they are ill-prepared, such as extreme rock climbing or rafting, and accidents do happen. A *Survivor* participant was recently admitted to hospital with serious burns and a *Wipeout* participant suffered a stroke ("Is Reality TV Too Cruel?" 2012). Other shows depict people in dangerous situations, committing crimes such as drunken driving or underage drinking and it would seem to be unclear as to what kind of legal obligation, if any, producers might be under to protect the individual. This is a point echoed by Wyatt (2009) who emphasizes that contestants are largely unprotected by basic workers' rights. Indeed, working conditions may be intentionally worsened to provoke extreme reactions, the key to successful reality TV. Much needed legislation has been introduced successfully in some countries, but if pushed too far, this might be interpreted as state interference in public entertainment. A case in question is the recent decision by China to limit the number of reality TV shows to two a week per network ("China to limit", 2011). More could still be done to protect individuals against possible dangers.

Despite the questionable ethics of reality TV, there are some critics who consider it to have social and educational merits. Poniewozik (2013), for example, favours watching competition shows with his family. He claims that by viewing the world through others' eyes and experiences you gain unexpected new insights. For instance, following a business startup show, he realized "what a fascinating process conceiving and valuing a business is" (p. 54). Nevertheless, his principal motivation for watching would still appear to be a good evening's entertainment, not to receive an educational experience. Ouellette (2010) recognizes that reality TV is melodramatic, but still argues for its civic value in promoting self-empowerment, inspiration for volunteerism and charity in shows, such as *Extreme Makeover* and the *Secret Millionaire*. This point is supported by a recent survey from the American Girl Scout Research Institute of girls aged 11 to 17, where 75% agreed that "the shows depicted people with different backgrounds and beliefs", and 62% that "they raised their awareness of social issues and causes".[2] This could also help address discrimination, encourage tolerance and normalize co-operation between social groups that are divided by gender, race, ethnicity and sexual

---

[2]   The Girl Scout Research Institute (6–26 April 2011). The survey was conducted by the research firm TRU and consisted of a sample of 1,141 girls aged 11–17.

orientation. Some argue though that these shows could still do more to challenge stereotypical representations (Sears and Godderis, 2011; Bell-Jordan, 2008) and racial division (Rothman, 2012). Ultimately, any possibility for social and educational benefit should be weighed carefully against the findings from studies revealing negative influences. For instance, the Girl Scout Research Institute survey (see above) indicates that the same girls who claimed to be inspired by reality shows seemed also to have gained an inaccurate understanding of social norms and acceptable behaviour from their viewing.

Undeniably, reality TV has over the last ten years become a popular expression of contemporary global culture, one which certainly could help bring about learning and good citizenship. However, in order to satisfy ratings and turn profits, these shows are heavily driven by the need to entertain rather than the need to educate or encourage social values and this, in turn, can impact audiences and participants negatively. Very few people switch on a reality show wanting to learn how to cook the perfect pavlova or to start a business on £150; rather, we watch to enjoy the public humiliation of an amateur cook with a collapsed soufflé or the dramatic boardroom shaming of an over-confident business hopeful. Like the Roman amphitheatre, reality TV is predominantly satisfying popular demand for uncomplicated sensation and entertainment with less concern for morals, ethics or taste. Its future depends on whether it continues to seek the largest possible audience, whether states apply censorship to control its excesses, or whether its potential merits are exploited to promote social harmony.

References:

Bell-Jordan, K. E. (2008) Black white and a survivor of the real world: Constructions of race on reality TV. *Critical Studies in Media Communication* 25 (4): 353–372.

Britain's Got Talent final thrashes *The Voice* in ratings war (14 May 2012). *The Telegraph*. Retrieved from: http://www.telegraph.co.uk/culture/tvandradio/britains-got-talent/9264294

China to limit 'vulgar' reality television shows (26 October 2011). BBC News Asia. Retrieved from: http://www.bbc.co.uk/news/15459367

Is Reality TV Too Cruel? [Editorial] (14 May 2012). *Scholastic Scope* 60 (13): 20–21.

Ouellette, L. (2010). Reality TV gives back: On the civil functions of reality entertainment. *Journal of Popular Film and Television* 38 (2): 66–71.

(The remaining references have been taken out to save space.)

Write a report on reality TV describing children's viewing habits, then focusing on two particular areas of concern and ways in which these issues could best be addressed.

Introduction

Not long ago, children were raised on a diet of *Sesame Street*, *Disney* and *Scooby Doo*, with the occasional sitcom and wildlife programme. Parents were secure in the knowledge that their youngsters were exposed to nothing unsuitable, and might possibly learn something too. Today, the situation has radically changed. Reality TV (RTV) has replaced the old sitcom at the top of the TV ratings (Nielsen, 2011), appealing to broadcasting networks with its popular and cheap to produce content. Digital access to hundreds of channels on demand makes these shows more accessible, whilst presenting new challenges for parents. This report maintains that the amount of RTV children are watching is a serious concern, particularly in light of the growing number of online multimedia viewing options. It begins by examining recent statistics relating to children's RTV viewing, then moves to consider two particular areas of concern. Finally, it considers ways broadcasting networks, governments and parents might best address these issues.

1. Children's viewing habits

Various polls indicate that children, young and old, are watching a worrying amount of television, in particular RTV, most of which was originally designed for adults. According to the UK-based Broadcaster's Audience Research Board, BARB (2011), most of youngsters' viewing occurs noticeably *outside* traditional children's airtime, peaking between 20:00–20:30, and this is true of both older and younger children. It is no surprise then that reality TV constitutes a large proportion of the TV diet for children of all ages. In fact the same BARB report states that it actually accounts for five out of six of 10 to 15-year-old children's favourite shows in the UK (see Figure 1 below). These statistics lead both experts and parents to question its potential impact on children.

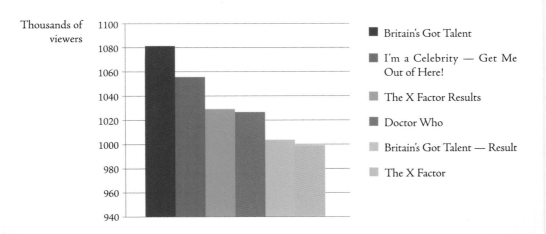

Figure 1: Top 6 TV shows, 2011, all children aged 10–15. Source: BARB, 2011. (Reality shows are shaded green.)

2. Potential issues in children's viewing of reality TV

The issues surrounding children's viewing of RTV are complex. This report focuses on two key areas: the difficulties children have connecting the reality they see on TV with the reality in their own lives, and the unlimited, unmonitored access to RTV afforded by new media.

2.1 Inability to distinguish between reality and fantasy

Research suggests that younger children, especially those under eight, are less able to differentiate between reality and fantasy than their elders (UMHS, 2013). As a result, they may accept the graphic images, violent language and contrived scenarios of RTV as reflections of "real" life, causing nightmares and leading them to imitate aggressive behaviour (AAP, 2001). Teenagers too are often unaware of the degree to which reality is manipulated. In a recent survey of girls aged 11–17 from the Girl Scout Research Institute (2011), 75% believed that competition shows and 50% that real-life shows are "mainly real and unscripted". This demonstrates a failure to understand the degree to which reality TV is edited and constructed. Furthermore, the girls' agreement with certain statements (see Figure 2) implies they both expect and are more tolerant of what might be termed "negative characteristics" than girls who do not watch RTV regularly.

> "Gossiping is a normal part of a relationship between girls" (78% vs. 54%)
>
> "It's hard for me to trust other girls" (63% vs. 50%)
>
> "You have to lie to get what you want" (37% vs. 24%)
>
> **[% watching show vs. % not watching show]**

Figure 2: "Varying perceptions of girls who watched and didn't watch RTV." Source: Girl Scout Research Institute (2011).

Although the same girls (see above) could recognize that many shows set a negative example, and some of the above figures might look relatively low, this does still indicate that a significant proportion of youngsters have unhealthy views as a consequence of watching RTV.

2.2 Unlimited access to inappropriate shows

It is not just what youngsters watch but also how they watch and for how long that concerns many parents. Rideout et al. (2010) state that two-thirds of US children have televisions in their bedrooms for unsupervised viewing. Whilst this is worrying, even more disturbing is the recent US statistic that 8 to 18-year-olds' combined average media use (cell phones, iPods, laptops, etc.) increased from 6.21 hours a day in 2004, to 7.38 in 2009 and that the largest part of this is spent watching TV, which is actually equivalent to an adult's full working week (Kaiser Foundation, 2010).

It is unlikely that many parents know exactly what their children are watching unmonitored on these new platforms, although considering youngsters' RTV preference (see Figure 1), one might presume they are watching similar shows, as well as more inappropriate RTV originating from later time slots. This is why finding ways to regulate RTV content and educate children about its shortcomings must be a priority.

3. Addressing the issues

This section will consider a range of ways to address two issues: confusion of reality and fantasy and unlimited access to inappropriate shows.

3.1 Helping children distinguish between reality and fantasy

By watching RTV together as a family, parents can make an important contribution, engaging their children in critical conversation that helps them recognize how "reality" is constructed in these shows and is therefore essentially "unreal". This would encourage "active viewers" rather than a "passive audience" (Holmes, 2004). Talking about the real-life consequences of immoral behaviour and comparing television reality with their own reality can help children apply what they have seen to their own lives in a healthier way. Schools might also play a role, teaching children to analyze content, for instance, by debating moral issues from the shows in Media Studies classes. Professional organizations such as the Parents' Television Council (2012) and The University of Michigan Health System (2013) provide useful web-based resources to support parents and schools in encouraging children to engage in this way.

3.2 Tackling the issue of unlimited access to inappropriate shows

This is a complicated issue with a range of responses, from direct censorship, to various parental measures.

3.2.1 Governments and broadcasting networks: Tighter regulations

External monitoring and legislation are two extreme ways of ensuring appropriate content, especially when children are most likely to be watching. Some networks have disputed the regulatory approach, as did Fox TV unsuccessfully in 2012 (Flint and Savage, 2012). In China, the State Administration of Radio, Film and Television has limited satellite channels to two reality programmes a week ("China to limit", 2011), and in India, two shows with "vulgar language" and "objectionable scenes" were moved to a later slot (Burke, 2010). Although such censorship is problematic in a free society and it also does not completely solve the problem of unlimited access on mobile devices, in passing tighter regulations, governments are, nevertheless, communicating a vital message to broadcasting networks to be more careful about content.

3.2.2 Parental measures: Internet filters, setting time limits and educating by example

Whilst legislation can have its uses, it is almost certainly parents who have the greatest potential to bring about change. It is highly advisable they are familiar with the latest RTV programme content to exercise informed control over their children's viewing. One way of doing this is by studying networks' own ratings. The US television industry, for instance, has a ratings system which can be linked to a V-chip, allowing parents to block unsuitable programmes. In addition to this, anxious parents can utilize a wide range of parental control software (e.g. NetNanny, Netflix and Hulu) to block offending programmes, or alternatively, they can block access altogether to the TV and Internet at certain times of the day.

The above measures all relate to parental controls, it is essential, however, that parents also take a proactive role in setting a good example. For instance, given that parental programme choices are known to strongly influence those of their children (Parents Television Council, 2012), they should select their own viewing carefully. Similarly, they should limit their viewing and switch off unsuitable RTV shows, whilst explaining why they are doing so. Further positive habits could be fostered by encouraging children to participate in healthier activities such as sports, drama and music, and engaging in these as a family sometimes too.

Conclusion

Reality TV has established itself in global culture, and children everywhere will continue to be exposed to it in the foreseeable future. The problems many children have responding appropriately to adult-oriented content are very real, and aggravated further by today's pervasive Internet access. Various control mechanisms and efforts to improve critical awareness are needed. Parents are key to both, but schools, governments and broadcasting networks may have a part to play as well. Beyond this, more empirical research on the impact of the media on children's development would be useful in identifying content to be avoided.

References:

[AAP] American Academy of Pediatrics, Committee on Public Education (November 2001). Media violence. *Pediatrics* 108(5): 1222–6.

[BARB] Broadcasters' Audience Research Board (2011). Children's TV viewing: BARB analysis. Available from: http://www.barb.co.uk/

Burke, J. (18 November 2010). India's "vulgar" reality TV shows judged too real for viewers. *The Guardian*. Available from: http://www.theguardian.com/world/2010/nov/18/india-vulgar-reality-tv-shows

China to limit "vulgar" reality television shows (26 October 2011). BBC News Asia. Retrieved from: http://www.bbc.co.uk/news/15459367

Federal Communications Commission (2007). In the matter of violent television programming and its impact on children. Federal Communications Commission Washington, D.C. 20554. Retrieved from: http://www.c-span.org/pdf/fcc_tvviolence.pdf

(The remaining references have been taken out to save space.)

Task 3
Identify broad structure

Study the flow diagrams on pages 123–124 which establish the functions of each paragraph (essay) or section (report), including the stances (S), counter-arguments (C/A), rebuttals (R) and section headings/numbering (report). As a group, discuss the *similarities* and *differences* between the structures of the two pieces of writing. When you are ready, complete the table on page 125.

Essay structure:

Introduction

- Main focus of essay
- Background information
- Main stance
- Outline of structure

Stance 1

S: Moral issues (it is humiliating and deceptive)

C/A: It is acceptable if rules are known by all.

R: But it is not acceptable if people are openly deceived.

Stance 2

S: RTV is dangerous.

C/A: Legislation to protect against dangers may be criticized as "interfering".

R: But measures are still needed to protect people.

Counter-argument

C/A: RTV has educational and social merits.

R1: We watch mainly for entertainment, less for education.

R2: RTV is melodramatic.

R3: RTV could do more to challenge stereotypes and racial division.

R4: Unhealthy concept of socially acceptable behaviour among girls in the survey

Conclusion

- Restatement of main issue and stance
- Main arguments restated with vivid examples
- Future predictions

Report structure:

Introduction
- Background information
- Main focus of report
- Statement of main stance
- Outline of structure

1. Background Statistics
S: Children view too much RTV

2.1 Issue 1
S: Children have difficulty interpreting "RTV reality".
C/A: Teenage girls realized RTV set a bad example.
R: A significant number of youngsters still have unhealthy views on acceptable behaviour as a result of their viewing.

2.1 Issue 2
S: Unlimited, unmonitored access to RTV, particularly using digital media, is worrying. Children have difficulty interpreting "RTV reality".

3.1 Solution 1 (Issue 1)
S: Children should learn how to evaluate RTV "reality" critically with involvement from parents and schools.

3.2.1 Solution 2 (Issue 2)
S: Regulations/external monitoring need tightening.
C/A: This is problematic in a free society.
R: Legislation is still important.

3.2.2 Solution 3 (Issue 2)
S: Parents need to be actively involved with controls and education.

Conclusion
- Restatement of situation
- Summary of stance and key issues
- Future recommendations

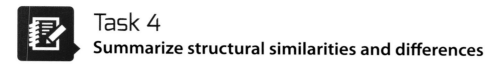

Task 4

Summarize structural similarities and differences

Now complete the sentences below with *similarities* and *differences* between the structure of the above essay and report.

Similarities in structure	Differences in structure
1. Both texts begin with an _____ and end with a _____	1. The report has headings, _____ and a _____ system to facilitate comprehension. The essay uses _____ sentences for this purpose.
2. Both texts contain a clear _____ with two main _____	2. After presenting the two main arguments, the report has a section covering _____, whilst the essay has a paragraph of _____.
3. Both texts contain _____ and _____ to balance the main arguments.	3. The report has an additional section after the introduction giving _____ _____. This kind of information is presented in the essay's _____.

Think again: The above sentences refer to the specific essay/report you read earlier. Tick "✓" those features which you would expect to find in **most** other essays/reports. You can use the table below to help you.

This table summarizes some of the key structural differences you have seen between essays and reports.

Academic essay	Academic report
Paragraphs	**Sections**
The main building blocks of an academic essay are its paragraphs. Paragraphs are normally organized around one main stance with supporting examples or evidence. They also often contain counter-arguments and rebuttals to reflect the complexity of academic issues. Paragraphs have a clear internal structure and are held together with cohesive devices.	The main building blocks of an academic report are its sections, each of which covers one main idea. A section may consist of several shorter paragraphs known as "subsections", each covering one aspect of the same main idea. To help the reader follow more easily, it is common practice to add a sentence at the start of the section to summarize the section's main ideas.

Topic sentences	Headings and subheadings
Paragraphs in academic essays use topic sentences to summarize their stance. Sometimes these refer backwards to an idea in the previous paragraph before introducing the new stance. Topic sentences that begin with an example or citation should be avoided; it is important to express the stance in your own words.	Headings in academic reports work in a similar way to topic sentences in essays, focusing on the main idea and stance of the section. They should be kept as short as possible. Always remember to number them correctly and to use consistent font and spacing around them.

Task 5
Identify the functions of introductions and conclusions

Read the introduction and conclusion from your text again. Highlight and note down (on the text itself) the *functions of the sentences*. After this, record what you noticed in the table below and compare with the two students who read the other text. When you have finished, complete the two statements at the end.

Academic essay: Introduction	Academic report: Introduction
• Opening statement: introduces essay focus	• Background information: compares past/now
•	•
•	•
•	

Academic essay: Conclusion	Academic report: Conclusion
•	•
•	•

Both introductions in this unit include: ....

Both conclusions in this unit include: ....

Summary of features of academic introductions and conclusions

Academic introductions and conclusions are both crucial in telling the reader the focus and main ideas of an academic essay or report. The following is a summary of some of the most common features.

Introduction

Do not underestimate the value of your introduction, as the "gateway" to your writing. **Most** introductions will:

- introduce the **main focus** of the report or essay
- provide **background information** to gain an initial insight into the topic, e.g. statistics, comparisons, useful facts, expert quotes or theory
- express the **main stance** of the essay; the **main stance/findings** in a report
- outline the **structure** and **purpose** of the essay or report

Introductions **may** also:

- highlight the **complexity/significance** of the topic
- define **key terms**
- mention **scope** or **limitations** (particularly reports)

Tip: Try to stay away from questions directly addressing the reader. Students often write these in the wrong tone, and the questions themselves tend to be too general and not very interesting.

Conclusion

The conclusion brings together the whole text. It helps reinforce the key ideas and **usually** includes:

- **restatement of the stance:** after presenting all the arguments in the body paragraphs and sections, the conclusion reminds the reader of the main stance.
- **summary of key points:** the conclusion also summarizes key points to remind readers of the arguments for the stance.

It may also include mention of limitations or scope. Typically, it may end with:

- **prediction** or open question about the future
- **discussion of the future implications** of the stance
- **recommendation** for further **action or research** (common in reports)

Tip: Avoid adding any new ideas in the conclusion.

Task 6

Create links backwards and forwards between sections

The previous unit introduced a range of devices such as lexical repetition, referencing and connecting devices that are used to make links between ideas *within* a paragraph or section. Similar techniques are also used *between* paragraphs or sections to create a web of connections across wider stretches of text. These references most often point *backwards*, but they can also look *forwards* to information which will follow. Such strategies can easily go by unnoticed. This section will highlight two ways in which this effect can be achieved.

Topic and final sentences

Topic and final sentences most commonly introduce or summarize the stance of the paragraph/section in question, though they do have some additional functions.

Topic sentences: Locate the following two topic sentences in this unit's essay and report. What strategy do they both use? Complete the descriptions in the two boxes.

> "Humiliation and deception are definitely a concern, but more worrying is the effort some shows go to in search of new and often dangerous ways to maintain audience ratings." (essay, paragraph 3)

> "Whilst legislation can have its uses, it is almost certainly parents who have the greatest potential to affect change." (report, section 3.2.2)

1. The first part of the sentence (**before** the comma) refers to:

    _____

2. The second part of the sentence (**after** the comma) refers to:

    _____

Final sentences: Now look at the report and locate the following two final sentences. How do they create a link forwards?

> "These statistics lead both experts and parents to question its potential impact on children." (section 1)

> "This is why finding ways to regulate RTV content and educate children about its shortcomings must be a priority." (section 2.2)

Reference to data and sources

In academic writing, it is often necessary to refer to the same data, study or source several times in one text. This is particularly true of reports that have a lot of data or diagrams. Complete the table with an example for each type of reference and the section/paragraph number in which you found it.

Type of reference	Example	Location
a. Backwards reference to statistics		report, section ......
b. Backwards reference to a study		essay, paragraph .....
c. Forwards reference to a diagram		report, section ......

Task 7
Write a group report

At the start of their studies, students typically have had more practice writing essays than reports. Therefore, this book's final writing practice focuses on the structural features of an academic report. You will be writing a group report on the following topic:

> **Write a report on teenagers' use of technology today. Highlight two areas of particular concern and suggest which measures might be the most effective in overcoming this situation.**

Procedure for writing your group report

Step 1. Identify arguments and examples: Form a group of five. Underline key words in the task question (see above), then skim through Daniela's notes on page 131 and identify which parts relate to *"concerns about technology"* and which parts to *"measures for overcoming the situation"*.

Step 2. Write a plan: As a group, complete the following report plan using some of the arguments and examples you identified in Step 1. Include your *stance*, *counter-arguments* and *rebuttals* as well as *section headings* and *numbering*. Select arguments and examples. You do not need to include all of Daniela's ideas.

Plan: Report on Teenagers' Use of Technology

Introduction

-

-

-

-

1. Negative impacts of teenagers' technology use

1.1

1.2

2. Measures to address the problem

2.1

2.2

Conclusion

-

-

Daniela's notes on Teenagers' Use of Technology

Background on SNSs (Social Media / Networking Site = SMS / SNS)

- "Teens represent the leading edge of mobile activity". *Mary Madden, Senior Researcher, Pew Research Project (2013) [Internet]*
- Facebook (SMS): reached one billion users on Sept. 14, 2012 *(Fowler, 2012)*.
- ➤ UK National Survey "Ofcom" (2012). Children aged 12-15: 100% children used Internet, 80% used social networking sites, they spent 17.1 hours a week online.
- ➤ China, 26th Stat. Survey Report Internet Development in China, 2010: 420 million Internet users – 29.9% of these = teens, aged 10-19 *(Huang & Leung, 2012)*.

---

1. Issue 1: Social Networking (SNSs) → Cyberbullying

Problem:
Public SN profiles → children vulnerable – online bullying & inappropriate content:

☹ Microsoft Online Bullying Survey (2012):

- Ave.: 37% children (aged 8-17) worldwide report bullying online
- 54% children worldwide (aged 8-17) & 3 in 4 parents/educators worried about bullying online

Causes:

- Many teens X using privacy settings.
- Parents X monitoring children online.

But ☺ Social Networking → improved well-being (C/A)

☺ Study of 344 Spanish teens = SNSs increase self-esteem, decrease loneliness (Apaolaza, 2013).

But: same article says effort still needed to stop teens posting neg. comments.

Solutions:
1. Improve teacher training, info. at school e.g. Microsoft's training programme in European schools (Microsoft.com, 2013) – 23% UK teachers said X enough e-safety training (Aston & Brzyska, 2012).
2. Add abuse report button to SNSs, force oblig. use of real name, use more SNSs moderators etc. (Lee, 2013).
3. Parents: improve supervision & communication with children, report bullying.

---

2. Issue 2: Computer games → health concerns

Problem 1. Illness & behaviour problems

☹ Technology usage → teens w. late development, diabetes, obesity, damaged brain nerves, social problems and anger problems. (Mazmi et al., 2013)

☹ Correlation between Internet addiction & BMI (Canan et al., 2013).

Problem 2. Cognitive Development

☹ Children should be playing outside, physical activity. Deprivation → mental develop ↓
Ave. children (aged 10-11) = 2,000 hours at computer in one year. Addictive & can damage brain. (Baroness Greenfield, former director Royal Institution, 2011).
Attention shortage (Mazmi et al., 2013)

But ☺ Computer games → health improvements (C/A)

☺ Uni of Utah study (2012): interactive video games can benefit patients w. life-threatening illnesses, e.g. cancer, obesity, asthma, depression etc.
☺ Can ↓ stress and depression in "Type A" personalities (Vedantam, 2009).

But: Aren't these exceptions to the rule? Studies warning of dangers seem more numerous.

Solutions:
- Educators: Balance computer-based activities with outdoor ones, promote sport & health in schools.
- Govt. sport activities subsidies – e.g. UK Govt Report, 2013 – programmes & facilities to keep Olympic Legacy, 2012 alive ("Inspired by 2012", 2013).

Step 3. Write your individual section: Each student in your group should now write one of the main sections, but not the conclusion. Distribute the work equally among the members of your group.

Step 4. Put it together: Put your group's sections together to form one text. You can use a computer or scissors and glue to do this. As a group, write a simple conclusion which reflects the points covered in the sections. After this, check that your report makes sense as a whole. Check features of text structure such as topic and final sentences, links between sections, organization of ideas, as well as backwards and forwards references across sections.

Step 5. Give feedback: Exchange your report with that of another group. Read the other report and give feedback on it using the checklist below. Add "✓" if the criteria is fulfilled, and "?" if you feel an improvement is needed. Finally, add two suggestions for improvement.

	✓ or ?
Introduction and conclusion Are the key elements present: background, stance and an outline (introduction); restatement of stance and summary of main points (conclusion)? Is the conclusion free of new ideas?	
Broader structure including headings, subheadings, numbering Is there a logical structure? Does the report have suitable headings and subheadings with an accurate numbering system? Do the main sections have an introductory sentence?	
Topic and final sentences Do all sections have effective topic and final sentences? Do the topic sentences use the writer's own words and not start with an example?	
Sequence of information within a paragraph Is there a logical flow of information: stance – example/evidence – interpretation?	
Arguments, counter-arguments and rebuttals Are there some counter-arguments and rebuttals?	
Links backwards and forwards Does the report hang together well with references to previous ideas and to ideas that are still to come? Does the report use topic sentences, final sentences and pronoun referencing to link backwards and forwards?	

Two suggestions for improvement:

-

-

Homework

Prepare for a tutorial discussion

Teenagers' use of the Internet and technology is a controversial topic nowadays that receives a lot of attention globally. In the following tutorial discussion, you will share your views on the topic and consider which measures might be taken to minimize potential issues. Discuss the following questions:

1. In your opinion, do the Internet and technology do more harm or good to teenagers?

2. What should schools, governments and parents do in the future to ensure that students most benefit from/have a positive experience of the Internet and technology?

ACADEMIC SPEAKING

Task 1
Review discussion strategies

This final discussion unit will give you the opportunity to review what you have learnt in the previous units about discussion strategies. It will allow you to reflect upon your progress and consider how you might continue to develop this skill in future discussions. First, read the following 10 tips and evaluate your performance now at the end of the course. Tick "✓" the boxes on a scale of 1–3.

1 = I do this well most of the time; **2** = I do this well sometimes; **3** = I rarely do this well

10 tips for academic discussions	1	2	3
1. Preparation for the discussion: It is easy to underestimate the need for thorough preparation. Some students may skim texts quickly, failing to think critically about what they have read. Without careful selection of sources, skilful note-taking and genuine engagement with the ideas in your texts before the tutorial, it will be difficult to have a thought-provoking discussion. Try comparing yourself to a lawyer who is preparing for a court case, looking for one exceptional piece of evidence. Do the same when preparing for a discussion. Look for examples or angles that other students will notice and which could take the discussion to deeper levels.	☐	☐	☐
2. The power of questions: If we are to gain new and deeper understanding of an issue, we need to ask questions both of ourselves and of others. We have seen that questions can have many different functions in a discussion. To recap, here are just a few of them. • Ask yourself wh-questions to check you are covering a variety of perspectives. • Ask other participants questions to clarify meaning, to ask for additional information, to show polite disagreement and to check the reliability of content and sources. • Encourage a quiet participant to join the discussion with a friendly question. • Use a short tag question at the end of a turn, e.g. "Isn't it?", "Wouldn't you agree?" to check whether other participants agree with you or not. • Ask open-ended questions if the discussion is moving too fast without sufficient depth.	☐	☐	☐

3. Active listening: Do you ever have the feeling that someone is not genuinely listening? Perhaps they are too busy "rehearsing" their next move, perhaps they are listening "selectively", or perhaps they are simply thinking of something else. Active listeners are fully present and will respond to *what they hear* rather than what they had *hoped* to hear. They will not simply "parrot" what was said before them, wasting time and adding nothing new; they also will not say "I agree" then change topic to something unconnected. Instead, they will comment on what was said previously and logically follow on from it. They may also jot down key points to refer back to later. Active listeners are valued since they show respect towards others, they are better able to synthesize ideas and their contributions tend to help discussions move forward constructively.

4. Critical thinking: Do you enjoy considering an issue from different angles? Do you try to imagine what people in other situations might say or what knowledge from other contexts might bring to your topic? Are you able to imagine alternative scenarios or reasons? Do you regularly use questions to reflect and create your own meaning from what you read or hear? Do you both agree **and** disagree? All of the above are characteristics of critical thinkers. Without it, discussions are likely to remain superficial and unsatisfying.

5. Structure: Both individual turns and the broader discussion need some structure. **Individual turns** may be structured in a number of ways, but one common feature is that they tend to begin with a "response" to the previous speaker. For example: *response – stance – example – interpretation*; *response – question*; *response – stance – question*; *response – summary – proposal of next topic*. At the broader **discussion level**, before launching into the main discussion, it is useful as a group to consider the question, agree on the points you will cover and what you aim to achieve. A good structure should not be so constraining that it stops you from examining unexpected ideas; it should be like a map that serves to keep the discussion on track.

6. Sources: Are you making the most of your sources and selecting them wisely? A good source should provide a number of examples and perspectives, as well as arguments and counter-arguments. Good sources are likely to inspire you and others to think about the issue in new ways. Ask yourself whether you tend to overuse or underuse sources. Students who use too many examples and very little of their own opinion will be hard to follow. Students who make big claims without any supporting evidence are likely to be considered unbelievable.

7. Body language: Imagine a discussion in which students never looked at each other or used non-verbal clues. It is hard to envisage how such a group would be able to work collaboratively, drawing connections and reaching new conclusions. Group work involves staying in touch with others. One of the main ways we do this is with body language, especially through eye contact with *all* group members, facial expressions and gestures like a nod of the head to signal attitude.

8. Be specific: Appropriate preparation should equip you with specific examples to help illustrate your point in a memorable and convincing fashion. Such examples may come from your own context, but they can also come from unfamiliar places and people, thus adding new dimensions to the discussion.

9. Making yourself heard: Do students often sit forward when you speak? Whilst this may be a sign of interest, it can be a sign that they are straining to hear you properly. Speaking in an academic discussion is different from chatting to a friend. You may well need to work harder to articulate your words clearly, to speak louder, to stress key words and to pause after these, too.

☐ ☐ ☐

10. Keeping it short: The time of a discussion is limited, as are people's attention spans. Good ideas can get lost or diluted by too many examples and unnecessary examples. Less is more.

☐ ☐ ☐

Task 2
Reflect on your discussion skills

In this task, you will reflect upon improvements you have made to your academic discussion skills during the course. After this, you will consider what area you could still improve and how you might achieve this. Use the following three guiding questions to examine your group's performance critically, bearing in mind the summary of strategies above. Afterwards, report back to the whole class on the three methods your group formulated in Question 3.

Reflect upon the following questions about academic discussion skills.

1. What have been the biggest improvements that you have made to your discussion skills during this course? How can this improvement be measured?

2. What do you think are the three areas that you and other students most commonly still find challenging? Why do you think this is? Give examples.

3. As a group, formulate one practical method that students could use to work on each of the three areas you have identified above. Record them below.

Method A:

Method B:

Method C:

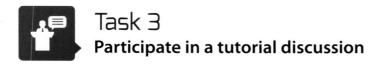

Task 3
Participate in a tutorial discussion

Now, hold a 30-minute tutorial discussion with your group members. The topic of your discussion addresses the following questions:

1. In your opinion, do the Internet and technology do more harm or good to teenagers?

2. What should schools, governments and parents do in the future to ensure that students most benefit from/have a positive experience of the Internet and technology?

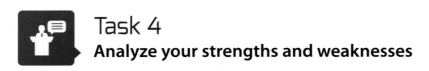

Task 4
Analyze your strengths and weaknesses

Take five minutes to fill in the form below. Rate your overall performance on each criterion as follows:

1 = I did this **most of the time**   **2** = I did this **some of the time**   **3** = I **rarely** did this

	1	2	3
My stance was:			
clear – e.g. I changed the written language in the source to my own spoken language.	1 ☐	2 ☐	3 ☐
concise – e.g. I expressed one idea at a time.	1 ☐	2 ☐	3 ☐
critical – e.g. I acknowledged that academic ideas are complex, not black and white.	1 ☐	2 ☐	3 ☐
I interacted well by:			
linking my ideas smoothly into the discussion – e.g. I linked my point to a point that had been mentioned before.	1 ☐	2 ☐	3 ☐
using active listening skills – e.g. I used eye contact, nodding, expressions of agreement.	1 ☐	2 ☐	3 ☐
not dominating – e.g. I allowed other students to break into the discussion.	1 ☐	2 ☐	3 ☐
My language was:			
fluent – e.g. I was able to speak without a lot of hesitations.	1 ☐	2 ☐	3 ☐
accurate – e.g. I was able to use a range of grammar and vocabulary to express complex academic ideas.	1 ☐	2 ☐	3 ☐
clear – e.g. I used stress, intonation and pausing to express my meaning.	1 ☐	2 ☐	3 ☐
I cited:			
from sources to support my stance – e.g. I didn't just rely on my own personal opinion in the discussion.	1 ☐	2 ☐	3 ☐
by mentioning the reliability of my source – e.g. I mentioned that the information I cited came from a reliable source (*The Journal of XX*/The World Health Organization).	1 ☐	2 ☐	3 ☐
This Unit's Focus			
I was active in negotiating a clear structure and in keeping the discussion on track.	1 ☐	2 ☐	3 ☐
I referred to ideas both in the previous turn and further back in the discussion.	1 ☐	2 ☐	3 ☐

Ideas for future improvement

Answers

Unit 1

ACADEMIC WRITING

 Task 4
Explore an argument in a written text

The table below outlines the key arguments in the essay and report.

Group A: Essay		Group B: Report	
Argument	Paragraph number	Argument	Section number
Opinions on the issue of healthcare are likely to be related to one's political views, ethical views, and socioeconomic status.	1	As countries rise out of poverty, their populations tend to develop a set of health conditions linked to their more affluent, urbanized lifestyle.	1
A combination of the two models is worth exploration and can serve as a blueprint for designing a more efficient healthcare system.	1	Levels of childhood obesity are growing.	2.1
The ability to pay for a higher cost healthcare system does not necessarily translate to better quality.	2	It is very difficult to compare rates of obesity across countries.	2.1
In order to better maintain other government-funded programmes, those who are able should take individual responsibility for their healthcare.	2	There are significant negative medical and non-medical consequences of obesity. However, the amount of research on the long-term effects of obesity is scarce.	2.2
In a government-paid system, the higher upfront costs that the government would accrue initially could be offset or eventually reduced by a decrease in the frequency of expensive emergency visits.	3	Individuals' increasing energy consumption and decreasing energy expenditure through a lack of exercise are the two main factors contributing to obesity.	3

But, while shifting to a government-provided healthcare system would increase coverage for those who cannot afford healthcare, new controversy and complexity would also be introduced.	3	There is little chance of DCs averting an obesity pandemic in the future.	4
A combined approach to funding healthcare is crucial.	4	DCs tend to have limited resources for large-scale intervention programmes through the public health sector and much of these populations associate a more "Westernized" lifestyle with an increase in social status and are therefore reluctant to give up habits which contribute to obesity.	4
		Although many of the underlying causes of obesity stem from much needed growth, for example, access to higher-paid employment in the service sector and increased economic wealth, interventions are needed, even if they have a limited effect in the near future.	4

 ## Task 5
Identify features of a successful academic essay or report

These are only suggested answers; other answers are also possible.

Essay Topic:

Who should pay for healthcare?

The issue of who should pay for healthcare is highly controversial and complex. **Opinions on this issue are likely to be related to one's political views, ethical views, and socioeconomic status.** Funding for healthcare tends to come from four major sources: direct payment by the user, taxes from the public, national health insurance and private health insurance.

← Stance – shows complexity of topic

Upon closer investigation, these four sources can be further categorized into **a government-provided healthcare system** (taxation and national health insurance) and **a user-paid system** (private health insurance and direct payment by the user at the time of treatment). This essay will first discuss these two models of healthcare and afterwards **argue that a combination of the two models is worth exploration and can serve as a blueprint for designing a more efficient healthcare system.**

People from wealthy backgrounds tend to support **a user-paid system** based on the belief that this type of system provides more choice and better quality than a government-run system. However, an examination of the overall US healthcare model illustrates that this is often not true. Davis et al. (2007) report that **"despite having the most costly health system in the world, the United States consistently underperforms on most dimensions of performance, relative to other countries"** (p. 34). The ability to pay for a higher cost healthcare system does not necessarily translate to better quality. **Another major argument** for a user-paid system is that it is an individual's responsibility to pay if the individual has the funds to do so. Otherwise, government revenue would be required, which is also needed for a number of other critical public programmes such as education and new infrastructure. Therefore, in order to better maintain other government-funded programmes, those who are able should take individual responsibility for their healthcare. While this point is valid, **the question of how those with insufficient economic means will be able to get healthcare remains unanswered.**

A controversial solution to **this question** lies within **a government-provided healthcare system**. One clear benefit to government funding is that those who cannot afford healthcare are provided with it. If a large percentage of any population cannot afford medical care, productivity among that population would likely decrease in cases of illness. There is also research to suggest that people who have constant access to healthcare generally live healthier lives and cost the medical system less overall than those who go to the doctor only in an emergency (**Williams 2005; Emerson 2006**). The higher upfront costs that the government would accrue initially could be offset or eventually reduced by a decrease in the frequency of expensive emergency visits. An illustrative example of this was highlighted by Gawande (2011), who describes a preventative programme in the US that resulted in net savings in healthcare costs that were "undoubtedly lower" (para. 39). **However, arguments against a government-paid system still persist.** According to Smith (2001), it is often politically unpopular, as governments need to increase taxation as the population ages. This would

Organization – two points of focus of essay

Stance – overall thesis of essay

Organization – first focus of essay

Citation – direct quote to support stance

Organization – second argument in paragraph

Organization – use of pronouns to show connections with the essay

Organization – second focus of essay

Citation – evidence from multiple sources to support stance

Stance – putting both sides of the argument to give a balanced and complex argument decrease the likelihood of success for governments to convince people that a largely government-run system would be cheaper and more efficient. Few politicians would want to damage their own political careers by instituting higher taxation. **Thus, while shifting to a government-provided healthcare system would increase coverage for those who cannot afford healthcare, new controversy and complexity would also be introduced.**

Organization – a summary sentence at the end of the paragraph

In light of the benefits and deficiencies mentioned above, advocacy for a combined approach to funding healthcare is crucial. In fact, successful examples of a merger between the two healthcare systems are already existent. Hong Kong operates both a government- and user-paid healthcare system, broadening coverage for the entire community while maintaining more personalized services and choices for those who are able to afford them ("HK healthcare is a dual-track system", 2013). **The same article also notes impressive and comparable measures of health in Hong Kong, with an infant mortality rate below 2 deaths per 1000 live births and an 80-year life expectancy.** In a similar comparison, Singapore employs a combined healthcare system. This combination has allowed Singapore to ensure health coverage for the poor, prevent financial destitution from catastrophic illness, and still preserve choices for those more financially able (Lim, 2004). **Health outcomes indicate efficacy: a 78.4 years in life expectancy, 2.2 per 1000 infant mortality rate, and an 80% satisfaction rate for corporatized public hospitals (Lim, 2004).** However, it should be noted that Hong Kong and Singapore have unique social and economic situations, and a population that, in contrast with other developed nations, is significantly smaller and more manageable. Nonetheless, they can be used as starting points for how a combined approach to healthcare can be administered as supported by Haseltine (2013), a noted Harvard professor and AIDS researcher, who believes that an investigation of the Singaporean healthcare system should be a requisite when government officials debate issues concerning healthcare systems. This combined approach also helps to partially alleviate political concerns about taxes mentioned previously as KPMG International (2012) reports that Hong Kong and Singapore are among the lowest, globally, in personal income tax rates and have remained flat since 2004. Evidence from these countries is highly suggestive that a government-paid system in conjunction with a public-user-paid system, if implemented correctly and accordingly, can maintain the benefits and allay deficiencies in each of the systems operating individually.

Stance – establishing an argument based on points in previous paragraphs

Citation – statistics are given to strengthen stance

What is clear is that deciding which party is responsible for funding healthcare costs is highly contentious. In response, this essay has discussed the benefits and deficiencies of a government-paid healthcare system and a public-user-paid system. Despite the possibility of higher taxes and inadequate allocation to other government-funded programmes, a government-paid healthcare system offers coverage to a wider number of people. However, proponents of a public-user-paid system believe that healthcare should be the responsibility of each individual. **In view of these arguments, a way forward is to establish a feasible combined healthcare system approach.** Using Singapore and Hong Kong as case studies, other nations should investigate how this approach can be successfully applied to their local contexts in order to minimize weaknesses in each individual healthcare system while maximizing their benefits.

→ Stance – summary

References

Davis, C., C. Schoen, M. Schoenbaum, A. Doty, J. Holmgren, & K. Shea (2007). An international update on the comparative performance of American health care. *The Journal of International Health Education* 1(12): 125–204.

Emerson, A. (2006). Emergency care and its costs. *The Journal of Emergency Health* 2(24): 116–132.

Gawande, A. (2011, 24 January). The Hot Spotters: Can we lower medical costs by giving the neediest patients better care? *The New Yorker*. Retrieved from http://www.newyorker.com/reporting/2011/01/24/110124fa_fact_gawande?currentPage=all

Haseltine, W. A. (2013). *Affordable Excellence: The Singapore Healthcare Story*. Washington, D.C.: Brookings Institution Press.

Ko, W. M. (2013, 9 April). HK healthcare is a dual-track system.news.gov.hk. Retrieved from http://www.news.gov.hk/en/record/html/2013/04/20130409_190409.lin.shtml

KPMG International (2012). *KPMG's Individual Income Tax and Social Security Rate Survey 2012*. Retrieved from http://www.kpmg.com/global/en/issuesandinsights/articlespublications/documents/individual-income-tax-rate-survey-2012.pdf

Lim, M. K. (2004). Shifting the burden of health care finance: A case study of public–private partnership in Singapore. *Health Policy* 69(1): 83–92.

Smith, J. (2001). Politics and the tax system. *The Journal of Tax, Economics, and Politics* 3(21): 280–300.

Williams, A. (2005). Benefits of preventative care. *The Journal of Preventative Care and Medicine* 2(26): 200–220.

Report Topic:

How serious is the problem of childhood obesity in developing countries?
What are the causes? What are some possible interventions to lower obesity rates?

1. Introduction

The obesity epidemic has been "spreading" from developed to developing countries (DCs). As countries rise out of poverty, their populations tend to develop a set of health conditions linked to their more affluent, urbanized lifestyle. This phenomenon is not only being seen in adults, but increasingly in children too. <u>**This report will outline the seriousness of the childhood obesity problem in Asian DCs. It will then discuss the main causes of this problem**</u> and <u>**suggest a multifaceted approach to tackle this worrying public health problem.**</u>

> • Organization – outline of report
>
> • Stance – overall thesis of report

2. Seriousness of Childhood Obesity

2.1 Growing Levels of Childhood Obesity

Since there is currently no worldwide consensus regarding the definition of childhood obesity, it is very difficult to compare rates across countries. Different studies use different measures; some do not distinguish between being obese and overweight and some do. However, <u>**a common definition of childhood obesity is a BMI greater than the 95th percentile, while the definition of being overweight is greater than the 85th percentile for children**</u> [1].

> • Stance – definition of key terms to make stance clear

Despite differing measurements of obesity, some comparative research has been done to uncover trends in obesity in DCs. For example, one analysis of 160 nationally representative surveys from 94 DCs shows that obesity rates are increasing [2]. This phenomenon is mostly centred in urban areas of these countries [3] and the rates are much higher in older children (6–18) than in pre-schoolers [3].

<u>**For example, one study estimated that 12.9% of children throughout China were overweight and of those, 6.5% were obese [4]. However, urban areas usually have much higher rates than this. In Dalian, for example, the overweight rates (including rates of obesity) were found to be 22.9% for boys and 10.4% for girls [5].**</u>

> • Citation – statistics to strengthen stance

The rates for one urban area in India (Amritsar in the Punjab region) were slightly lower than in urban China: 14% of boys and 18.3% of girls aged 10–15 years were found to be overweight, and of those, 5% of boys and 6.3% of girls were obese [6]. The rate in Pakistan was similar: the overall rate of overweight and obesity in children was 5.7%. The rate in boys was 4.6% versus 6.4% in girls and these rates increased with age, rising to 7% and 11% for boys and girls aged 13–14 years [7].

These rates are not much different than those in the USA about 10 years ago. In 1998 the rates for 6 to 17-year-olds were 11% obese and 14% overweight [8]. Current rates are significantly higher, with 31.7% of the same age group overweight and 16.9% obese (2–19 years) [9]. This is an indicator of where many people in DCs might end up as they become more wealthy.

2.2 Consequences of Childhood Obesity
Severely overweight children are at risk of **developing skeletal [10], brain [11], lung [12] and hormonal [13] conditions.** Non-medical consequences are also severe. These include long-term effects on self-esteem, body image and also increased feelings of sadness and loneliness [14], largely as a result of peer rejection [15]. In severe cases, this rejection has been reported to lead to suicide [16]. The research into these long-term effects is scarce because high levels of childhood obesity are a relatively new phenomenon.

> Citation –
> evidence from
> multiple sources to
> support stance

3. Major Causes of Childhood Obesity
Malnutrition used to be the focus of public health initiatives in DCs. Now, while malnutrition is still a problem in these contexts, so too is obesity. This is largely caused by rapid urbanization [3] and increased wealth. This link between economic progress and negative health consequences, sometimes called "New World Syndrome" [3], is extremely complicated. **However, there are mainly two factors at play: individuals' increasing energy consumption and decreasing energy expenditure through a lack of exercise.**

> Organization –
> introducing two
> main causes which
> form the basis of
> sections

3.1 Increased energy consumption
The diet of people living in urban areas in DCs is vastly different from those living in rural areas [17] and includes consumption of a higher proportion of fat, sugar, animal products, and less fibre, often found in restaurant foods [17]. This diet leads to a higher consumption of energy than more "traditional" diets.

> Stance –
> headings
> which show writer's
> stance

3.2 Reduced energy expenditure
This increase in energy consumption is at odds with a decrease in

energy consumption. As a country moves from an agricultural economy to an industrialized one, the energy expenditure of the population tends to decrease [18]. There has been a lot of research about the effect of this trend on adult energy expenditure. Once industrial processes become more computerized, employment moves to the service sector and a larger proportion of the population spend the working day behind a desk, leading to lower levels of activity and ultimately higher rates of obesity. Less is known about children. However, **as noted in Section 2.2**, insufficient research has been conducted on childhood obesity, and thus the changes in DC youths' energy expenditure and the consequent impact on childhood obesity remains unclear.

Organization – references to previous sections to show links between ideas

4. Suggested Interventions

Unfortunately, there is little chance of DCs averting an obesity pandemic in the future [19]. There is no reason to believe that they will be any more successful than developed countries, which have been **largely unsuccessful** in reducing rates of childhood obesity. Furthermore, DCs tend to have limited resources for large-scale intervention programmes through the public health sector and much of these populations associate a more "Westernized" lifestyle with an increase in social status and are therefore reluctant to give up, for example, eating in restaurants, watching a lot of TV, playing computer games, and travelling predominantly by car.

Stance – clearly stated using evaluative language

However, this does not mean that action should not be taken. **Although many of the underlying causes of obesity stem from much needed growth, for example, access to higher-paid employment in the service sector and increased economic wealth, interventions are needed, even if they have a limited effect in the near future.** Kruger et al. [20] suggest a model for South Africa that can serve as a useful starting point for DCs. They argue that obesity prevention and treatment should be based on:

Stance – beginning of writer's stance to the 3rd question in the report topic

- education
- behaviour change
- political support
- adequately resourced programmes
- evidence-based planning
- proper monitoring and evaluation

They also argue that interventions should have the following components:
- reasonable weight goals
- healthful eating
- physical activity
- behavioural change

<u>**This model might sound vague, but this is necessary**</u> as the specifics of what programme to run or what kind of political change is needed will depend heavily on the target country and even target region within that country as each country and region has its own unique set of conditions which require different adaptations of these interventions.

Stance – acknowledging potential criticisms that a reader might make

5. Conclusion

<u>**Obesity has become a pandemic and the incidence of childhood obesity is rising in DCs. Its causes are complicated but they predominantly relate to the changing social and economic conditions which develop as countries gain wealth, urbanize and industrialize.**</u> In order to tackle this worrying trend, interventions which target local needs are needed. <u>**Even though medium-term success in lowering obesity rates is likely to be limited,**</u> meeting modest targets such as a reduction in 1–2% of childhood obesity can have a future impact on the health outcomes of millions of inhabitants of DCs.

Stance – summary

Stance – realistic recommendations are given

References

1. Must, A., & R. S. Strauss (1999). Risks and consequences of childhood and adolescent obesity. *International Journal of Obesity and Related Metabolic Disorders: Journal of the International Association for the Study of Obesity* 23 Suppl. 2: S2–11.
2. Onis, M., & M. Blossner (2000). Prevalence and trends of overweight among preschool children in developing countries. *American Journal of Clinical Nutrition* 72: 1032–1039.
3. Kelishadi, R. (2007). Childhood overweight, obesity, and the metabolic syndrome in developing countries. *Epidemiologic Reviews* 29: 62–76.
4. Wang, Y. (2001). Cross-national comparison of childhood obesity: The epidemic and the relationship between obesity and socio-economic status. *International Journal of Epidemiology* 30: 1129–1136.
5. Zhou, H., T. Yamauchi, & K. Natsuhara et al. (2006). Overweight in urban schoolchildren assessed by body mass index and body fat mass in Dalian, China. *Journal of Physiology and Anthropology* 25: 41–48.
6. Sidhu, S., G. Marwah, & Prabhjot. (2005). Prevalence of overweight and obesity among the affluent adolescent schoolchildren of Amritsar, Punjab. *Coll Antropol.* 29: 53–55.
7. Jafar, T. H., H. Qadri, M. Islam, J. Hatcher, Z. A. Bhutta, & N. Chaturvedi (2008). Rise in childhood obesity with persistently high rates of undernutrition among urban school-aged Indo-Asian children. *Arch Dis Child* 93: 373–378.
8. Troiano, R. P., & K. M. Flegal (1998). Overweight children and adolescents: Description, epidemiology, and demographics. *Pediatrics* 101(3): 497–504.
9. Ogden, C. L., M. D. Carroll, L. R. Curtin, M. M. Lamb, & K. M. Flegal (2010). Prevalence of high body mass index in US children and adolescents. *Journal of American Medical Association* 303(3): 242–249.
10. Dietz, W. H., W. L. Gross, & J. A. Kirkpatrick (1982). Blount disease (tibia vara): Another skeletal disorder associated with childhood obesity. *Journal of Pediatrics* 101: 735–737.

11. Scott, I. U., R. M. Siatkowski, M. Eneyni, M. C. Brodsky, & B. L. Lam (1997). Idiopathic intracranial hypertension in children and adolescents. *Am J Opth.* 124: 253–255.

12. Marcus, C. L., S. Curtis, C. B. Koerner, A. Joffe, J. R. Serwint, & G. M. Loughlin (1996). Evaluation of pulmonary function and polysomnography in obese children and adolescents. *Pediatr Pulmonol.* 21: 176–183.

13. Caprio, S., M. Bronson, R. S. Sherwin, F. Rife, & W. V. Tamborlane (1996). Co-existence of severe insulin resistance and hyperinsulinaemia in pre-adolescent obese children. *Diabetologia* 39: 1489–1497.

14. Strauss, R. S. (2000). Childhood Obesity and Self-Esteem. *Pediatrics* 105(1): 15.

15. Schwartz, M. B., & R. Puhl (2003). Childhood obesity: A societal problem to solve. *Obesity Reviews* 4 (1): 57–71.

16. Lederer, E. M. Teenager takes overdose after years of 'fatty' taunts. *The Associated Press*, 1 October 1997.

17. Popkin, B. M. (1998). The nutrition transition and its health implications in lower-income countries. *Public Health Nutr.* 1: 5–21.

18. Popkin, B. M. (2001). The nutrition transition and obesity in the developing world. *J. Nutr.* 131(3): 871S–873S.

19. Prentice, A. M. (2006). The emerging epidemic of obesity in developing countries. *Int. J. Epidemiol* 35(1): 93–99.

20. Kruger, H. S., T. Puoane, M. Senekal, & M. T. van der Merwe (2005). Obesity in South Africa: Challenges for government and health professionals. *Public Health Nutr.* 8: 491–500.

Task 8
Identify quality academic sources

These are only suggested answers; other answers are also possible.

Text	Good academic source?	Why or why not?
Text 1 – Book	Yes	Book is likely to be a good academic source as the book is edited by a university publisher and is recent. The content and language of the small excerpt is also in fairly objective and academic tone.
Text 2 – Website	No	Not a good academic source as the website is a commercial website, thus the research given in the website is likely to be bias. A commercial website selling its own products would be unlikely to publish information that damages their products.

Text 3 – Website	Yes	Written by a credible author. Also, the organization is a non-profit organization with experts in the field of health.
Text 4 – Journal Article	Yes	Journal articles are likely to be good academic sources because they go through a peer-reviewed editorial process.
Text 5 – Wikipedia	No	Wikipedia can be edited by anyone and thus does not go through a rigorous editorial process that checks the accuracy of the information.
Text 6 – Newspaper Article	Yes	The content and language appear to be objective. Most of the information in the article is sourced from a reputable organization.
Text 7 – Blog Entry	No	Site does not appear to be reliable and backed up by credible research. Language in the blog is also highly biased and the claims to research are not cited, which prevents the reader from assessing its academic suitability.

Task 10
Understand different types of supporting evidence

The table below shows the answers for whether the statements on the right are true or false.

1. **False**	The most common form of evidence used in academic writing is expert evidence through direct quotations.
2. **True**	Common knowledge and personal accounts are often not cited and come from the writer rather than academic sources.
3. **False**	To use expert evidence through quotations, you need to change the words in the original information.
4. **False**	Statistics are a type of evidence that can stand alone and does not need any explanation or interpretation.
5. **False**	Expert evidence through paraphrasing requires quotation marks and copying the same words that are used in the original information.

Task 11

Identify types of supporting evidence for your stance

The table below shows the type of supporting evidence that best describes each short excerpt.

Short excerpt	Where can you find this?	Type of supporting evidence
One clear benefit to government funding is that those who cannot afford healthcare are provided with it.	Essay; 3rd paragraph; 2nd sentence	Common knowledge
The rates for one urban area in India (Amritsar in the Punjab region) were slightly lower than in urban China: 14% of boys and 18.3% of girls aged 10–15 years were found to be overweight, and of those, 5% of boys and 6.3% of girls were obese [6].	Report; Section 2; 4th paragraph	Statistics
Nonetheless, they can be used as starting points for how a combined approach to healthcare can be administered as supported by Haseltine (2013), a noted Harvard professor and AIDS researcher, who believes that an investigation of the Singaporean healthcare system should be a requisite when government officials debate issues concerning healthcare systems.	Essay; 4th paragraph; middle of paragraph	Expert evidence through paraphrasing
Davis et al. (2007) report that "despite having the most costly health system in the world, the United States consistently underperforms on most dimensions of performance, relative to other countries" (p. 34).	Essay; 2nd paragraph; 3rd sentence	Expert evidence through quotations

ACADEMIC SPEAKING

Task 1
Consider the purpose of university tutorial discussions

These are only suggested answers; other answers are also possible.

Questions 1 and 2: Many answers are possible. It is perhaps important to consider the fact that university tutorial discussions, unlike debates, tend to be less about convincing others of your opinion, or of "winning" and more about working together, using critical thinking skills to reach deeper levels of understanding.

There is no one correct answer here. Some common challenges students face at the start of tutorial discussions include responding critically to others, expressing a complex stance, using their own words to express what they have read clearly, linking back to what other students have said, selecting sources wisely and integrating sources properly into their argument.

Task 2
Analyze discussion feedback

The boxes below use three different colours (as follows) to show: what the students did well, what they still need to improve and what the tutor's advice is on how they could improve.

Feedback for Student 1:

"You prepared well for this tutorial and made some effective notes. This helped you give some relevant examples to support your stance. Do you realize that you look down at your notes a lot though and that you speak very quickly, which can make it difficult to follow you? Don't forget to look at the other students as you speak and go a little slower. Perhaps you could ask questions occasionally to check students are with you."

Feedback for Student 2:

"You approached this tutorial seriously, were well-informed and did a good job of citing your sources clearly. I sometimes found it hard though to identify your stance. Remember, you shouldn't be trying to say everything you know, you need to be more selective. Practise recording your ideas in note form and organize them by topic and not the text. This way it should be easier for others to follow your position and to respond to you."

Feedback for Student 3:

"Well done. You managed to speak more loudly and clearly this time; you also made better eye contact and appeared more confident. I think you could disagree (politely) more and generally, be more critical of what you hear. Before the next discussion you might find it helpful to imagine what other people might say to help you consider alternative ideas and perspectives."

Feedback for Student 4:

"I noticed you balanced agreement and disagreement well this time, but I'm not sure that all your turns link properly to what the previous speaker said, e.g. if a question is asked, answer it first and then add your own stance, and if you change the topic, signal this too. You are using a good range of vocabulary, but you often forget to use modals and adverbs to state opinions cautiously, e.g. 'New students *might/ perhaps* need some time to adapt.'"

Unit 2

ACADEMIC WRITING

 ## Task 4
Look at a student's analysis

The following table shows an example of a student's analysis of the essay topic:

> **Compare and contrast Human Capital Theory and the Capabilities Approach and evaluate which has a more positive impact on society.**

Steps in analyzing an assignment topic	Application of these steps to a given topic
1: Circle the directive verbs and think about what they ask you to do.	Compare and contrast Human Capital Theory and the Capabilities Approach and evaluate which has a more positive impact on society. • *Compare* and *contrast* ask you to find similarities and differences. • *Evaluate* asks you to assess the two different approaches in terms of their impact on society and consolidate your own stance.
2: Underline the main content words and think about what they mean.	Compare and contrast <u>Human Capital Theory</u> and the <u>Capabilities Approach</u> and evaluate which has a more <u>positive impact on society</u>. • *Human Capital:* the skills, knowledge and attributes humans possess so they can perform labour which, in turn, produces economic value. *Human Capital Theory* supports the idea that investing in humans produces positive economic returns. • *Capabilities Approach:* unlike Human Capital Theory, this approach seems support the idea that we should focus investment in areas which develop human well-being rather than economic growth. • *Positive impact on society:* the report will need to look at the impact of these theories at the level of society (not just the individual) and will need to clearly convey which theory is more positive and why.

3: Think about what kind of information you will need to find in order to complete the assignment.	Use the information you generated in Steps 1 and 2 to help you complete this step. You will need to find: • *a range of sources which define the key terms in the report topic;* • differences and similarities (if any) between Human Capital Theory and the Capabilities Approach; • a range of viewpoints and examples relating to the impact of these theories on society;

4: Develop an outline for the report.	There is no one correct way of doing this. However, you need to ensure that the structure of your report will help you answer the assignment topic fully. Use your notes above to develop an outline for this report. You may wish to add subheadings or reduce/increase the number of headings given below:
	
	Here are two possible versions of an outline:
	
	Version 1
	1. Introduction
	2. Description of HCT
	3. Description of CA
	4. Pros of HCT and CA
	  • Case studies/egs
	5. Cons of HCT and CA
	  • Case studies/egs
	6. Conclusion
	
	Version 2
	1. Introduction
	2. Description of HCT
	  • Pros and cons of HCT with case studies/egs
	3. Description of CA
	  • Pros and cons of CA with case studies/egs
	4. Conclusion
	
	These headings will help you synthesize ideas later during the note-taking stage of the writing process.

5: Think about what kind of texts would have the information you need to support your stance in an academic way.	This kind of information is likely to be found in: • United Nations websites • NGO websites • books on approaches to allocating development aid • journal articles related to development theories • websites relating to the progress of the Millennium Development Goals

Task 8
Develop a note-taking style

Below is an example of a student's notes on the following essay topic:

> **Compare and contrast Human Capital Theory and the Capabilities Approach and evaluate which has a more positive impact on society.**

	HCT	CA
Defn./ background	• In past: investment in technology → economic growth . . . now • HCT believes investing in ppl → economic growth ◦ E.g. \$\$ allocated to education can ↑ economy after some time • Policymakers ☺ eco. growth ◦ ∴ p'makers often adopt HCT when making decisions • Uses "rate of return" as a measurement tool (Okene, 2006)	• <u>Capabilities Approach:</u> ≠ HCT, ∴ CA supports focus of investment in areas which ↑ human well-being rather than economic growth. • Looks @ developing humans' capabilities
Pros	• Investment in ppl can → economic growth → more economic benefits • Easy to model & quantify spending ◦ ∴ perceived as practical by donor agencies	• Human development is foregrounded over economic growth ◦ ∴ aid more likely to ↑ well-being • Developing capabilities→ ↑ achievement of things ppl want to do • Development more equitable • Ppl have greater control over their environments
Cons	• Simplistic ∴ cannot really model returns • Doesn't account for impact on gender/ well-being ◦ ∴ investment could ↓ overall well-being ◦ ∴ could be unethical	• Challenge: well-being = ??? ◦ ∴ difficult to identify ◦ ∴ difficult to know which capability sets to develop ◦ ∴ overwhelming for policymakers ◦ BUT Newman (2002) offers 10 core/global capabilities to assist decision makers.

Task 9
Develop a full draft

The following table will help you check your understanding of Katie's report.

Statement	True/False?
Katie believes that allocating aid towards human development is more important than allocating it towards economic development.	True
Katie believes economic development is likely to be one of several aspects which promote well-being.	True
Katie offers an example to help explain the Capabilities Approach.	True
Katie has written a "forward-looking" conclusion.	True

Task 10
Move from source texts to a paraphrase

As Katie writes her first draft, she needs to paraphrase. The table below shows how a student has identified key points in a source text through note-taking and then used these notes to develop a paraphrase.

Source text	Final version of Katie's notes	Paraphrased excerpt from Katie's report

A feature fundamental to Human Capital Theory is the role played by people in the development of economic growth, a chief objective of aid for policymakers adopting this approach. This theory positions humans as technology was positioned in the past: investing in technology (or humans in this case) has the potential to lead to economic returns. For instance, a national investment in free higher education or a regional endowment in a health and nutrition campaign has the potential to yield economic benefits.
 	
Consider the example of free higher education for a moment. In the instance that the costs associated with this intervention exceed the benefits, the rate of return to investment would be negative and thus, the investment would be deemed unwise within the HCT paradigm. This may occur in a country with high levels of graduate unemployment, for example. Policymakers would then find alternative ways to allocate their resources which would yield a positive rate of return.
 	
(Okene, 2006)
	2.1 Economic growth in Human Capital Theory (HCT)
	• Ppl "invested in" = Human Capital
	• Investing in ppl (e.g. edu/health/nutrition) → economic benefit for ind and society (Okene, 2006)
	• Returns on these ppl = rate of return (RoR) . . .
	  ○ this RoR ∴influences decision making
	  ○ e.g. if investing in edu → labour market productivity then investment is ☺ (Okene, 2006)
		2.1 Economic growth in Human Capital Theory (HCT)
		
		Despite the inclusion of the word "human" in the term, HCT in fact foregrounds economic growth as the core objective of development. Within this approach, it is believed that investing in people, through education, health and nutrition for example, will lead to economic benefits for individuals and society (Okene, 2006). This investment in people is termed "human capital" and the economic benefits derived from investing in this human capital are calculated as a rate of return.
		
		Decisions regarding whether to invest in developing higher-education systems within a country, for example, are therefore based on the rate of economic return. In other words, policymakers ask themselves the following question, "Will a given amount of public investment in higher-education resources yield a greater amount of returns in labour market productivity and worker earnings?" If the answer is "Yes", investment is justified within the HCT paradigm.

Task 13
Identify appropriate paraphrasing

The following notes explain the reasons why three short texts are well or poorly paraphrased.

Excerpt 1

Countries are now being more connected and interdependent culturally, economically and politically because of globalization. Economically, it has brought about an enormous increase in international trade and investment across different countries, leading to an increase in wealth and living standards for many countries. For instance, the average yearly income per person in China rose from $1460 USD in 1980 to $4120 in 1999.

☐ **Well paraphrased**   ✓ **Poorly paraphrased**

Reason:

Poorly paraphrased because the wording is very close to that in the source and the source is not acknowledged. Paraphrasing does not mean changing or reordering just a few words, or turning active voice into passive, or turning singular nouns into plural.

Excerpt 2

Globalization has improved the economy of some developing countries. An example is China, where average incomes have increased by more than half in just two decades (Houston, 2010) as a result of increased trade with and investment by foreign companies. This essay aims to examine the relationships between international trade and the economic growth of China in the past few decades.

✓ **Well paraphrased**   ☐ **Poorly paraphrased**

Reason:

Well paraphrased, because it shows that the student is able to express the cited ideas and data in his or her own words and that he or she is able to select relevant ideas and data to expand and support these in the writing.

Excerpt 3

Globalization often benefits Western companies, not the people in developing countries. The reason is that in many developing countries, Western companies are maximizing profits by using the cheap labour and raw materials (Kennett, 2012 in Houston, 2010). This essay will demonstrate that not all countries, or people within those countries, benefit from globalization equally.

☐ **Well paraphrased**   ✓ **Poorly paraphrased**

Reason:

Poorly paraphrased because the wording is very close to that of the source.

Task 14
Improve your paraphrase

The box below shows an example of a text which paraphrases a source document well.

> **Example paraphrase**
>
> There are both advantages and disadvantages to globalization. According to Houston (2010), increased international trade and investment has improved the living standards in many countries, such as China, which witnessed an increase of income per capita from $1460 USD in 1980 to $4120 in 1999. Nevertheless, Houston points out that not every country gains from globalization in the same way because in many third world countries, their inexpensive labour and natural resources are being exploited by Western companies.

ACADEMIC SPEAKING

Task 4
Identify the differences between spoken and written texts

The table below shows several key differences between written and spoken texts.

Categories	Written text	Spoken text
Grammatical structures	• Complex grammatical structures are often used. • Points can be re-read for clarification.	• Complex grammatical structures are usually simplified to enhance understandability. • Points are usually only uttered once.
Vocabulary	• Technical and/or complex vocabulary is often used.	• Technical/complex vocabulary is explained in simpler, more accessible language.
Signposting	• Information is often presented quite densely. • The reader can choose the pace.	• Information is communicated less densely to provide the listener with thinking time. • Signposting is often used to break up longer points, e.g. "the first/second/third point" etc.
Emphasis	• Italics/bold/underlining are sometimes used for emphasis.	• Stress/pause/pace are often used for emphasis.
Audience	• This varies quite a bit, but likely to be an academic audience for the sort of texts you read at university.	• Your peers, in the case of a tutorial discussion.

Unit 3

ACADEMIC WRITING

 Task 2
Analyze the language of a successful academic stance

The table below shows the changes that have been made to Mike and Jane's stances.

Change made	Mike	Jane	Stance is too personal/emotional, not reasonable, not justified and not critical.
	I think that embryo selection based on physical and mental traits is always a terrible idea!	I think that embryo selection based on physical and mental traits is always a great idea!	
Personal/emotional language changed to improve the **academic tone** of the stance	~~I think that~~ Embryo selection based on physical and mental traits is always ~~a terrible idea!~~ ethically unacceptable.	~~I think that~~ Embryo selection based on physical and mental traits is always ~~a great idea!~~ ethically acceptable.	
Hedging included to make the stance **more cautious**	Embryo selection based on physical and mental traits is **mostly** ethically unacceptable.	Embryo selection based on physical and mental traits is, **on the whole**, ethically acceptable.	
Justification of stance is included to make the stance **well-justified**	Embryo selection based on physical and mental traits is mostly ethically unacceptable **because it will lead to increased discrimination against the poor who will not be able to afford this type of technology**.	Embryo selection based on physical and mental traits is, on the whole, ethically acceptable **because parents have the moral responsibility to give their children the best opportunities in life they can afford**.	

Counter-argument and **rebuttal included** to make the stance **more critical**

Embryo selection based on physical and mental traits is mostly ethically unacceptable because it will lead to increased discrimination against the poor who will not be able to afford this type of technology. **Although it is argued that this type of technology will improve the life of individual children by giving them more opportunities, the effect on society as a whole will be more social inequality for people too poor to afford the technology and social instability.**

Embryo selection based on physical and mental traits is, on the whole, ethically acceptable because parents have the moral responsibility to give their children the best opportunities in life they can afford. **Although it has been claimed that this will lead to discrimination against people too poor to afford the technology, this is a reason to ensure that the technology is made accessible to as many people as possible through government control. Discrimination is not a reason to ban the technology itself.**

Stance is cautious, well-justified, critical and has an academic tone (not personal/ emotional).

Task 3
Identify and define a counter-argument and rebuttal

A counter-argument is an argument which argues against a stance.

A rebuttal is an argument which **argues against the counter-argument** and **therefore supports the original stance**.

Task 4
Identify stance in an academic essay

Stance is found throughout an essay, but it is found primarily in:

- the stance at the end of the introduction
- the topic sentences
- rebuttals
- the conclusion

Task 5

Identify the differences between three possible critical argument structures

The table below shows the missing elements.

	Structure One	**Structure Two**	**Structure Three**
Introduction	Stance	Stance	Stance
Paragraph 1	1st argument supporting stance	1st argument supporting stance	Counter-argument for stance + Rebuttal
Paragraph 2	2nd argument supporting stance	Counter-argument for 1 + Rebuttal	1st argument supporting stance + Counter-argument for 1 + Rebuttal
Paragraph 3	3rd argument supporting stance	2nd argument supporting stance	2nd argument supporting stance + Counter-argument for 2 + Rebuttal
Paragraph 4	Counter-argument for 1, 2 and 3 + Rebuttal	Counter-argument for 2 + Rebuttal	3rd argument supporting stance + Counter-argument for 3 + Rebuttal
Conclusion	Summary of stance and arguments 1, 2 and 3	Summary of stance and arguments 1 and 2	Summary of stance and arguments 1, 2 and 3

Two typical secondary school structures are:

	Structure 1	**Structure 2**
Introduction	Introduction of topic	Introduction of topic
Paragraph 1	Arguments **for** the topic	Theme 1 – Arguments **for and against** theme 1
Paragraph 2	Arguments **against** the topic	Theme 2 – Arguments **for and against** theme 2
Conclusion	Stance in a conclusion	Stance in a conclusion

The university-level structures:

- tend to have the stance at the beginning of the essay and this stance is then supported throughout the essay

- are longer and therefore have a more complex structure

- are more critical through the use of counter-arguments and rebuttals

 ## Task 6
Identify critical argument structure in an academic text

The argument structure in the essay matches **Structure Three**.

The table below shows the argument structure. Language used to signal the counter-argument and the rebuttal to the reader have been underlined.

ESSAY	Argument structure
Consider two cases. Michele and Michael have two embryos ready for implantation. Embryo A has XY sex chromosomes. Embryo B has XX. Should they be allowed to reject one embryo based on gender? Sex selection technology is currently being practised to varying degrees in many countries, although it is almost universally illegal. Consider the second case of Sally and Sam. Their embryo A has a gene that is linked to the propensity to be overweight, while B does not. Should they be allowed to reject embryo A? It is a possibility that tests in the future could identify a propensity (not 100% probability) to certain traits related to appearance, although this is not possible now. However, as we rush to gain a deeper understanding of the link between genetics and why some of us are more beautiful, more intelligent, etc., it is necessary to ask ourselves whether it is advisable to use pre/post-pregnancy technology for embryo/fetus selection of non-disease traits. <u>This essay argues that the use of such technology is unwise because it has the potential to cause greater harm than good for society as a whole, leading to an increase in social instability and inequality.</u> The issues raised in the two cases above will be used to support this stance throughout the essay.	← Stance

The main argument supporting the use of pre/post-pregnancy technology for non-disease states, such as gender and appearance, is that parents have the moral responsibility to "select" the best children that they could have based on the information available to them. One major proponent of this argument is Professor Savulescu, Uehiro Professor of Practical Ethics at the University of Oxford. He believes that "couples (or single reproducers) should select the child, of the possible children they could have, who is expected to have the best life, or at least as good a life as the others, based on the relevant, available information" (Savulescu, 2002, p. 415). He believes that technology should be used to give parents as much information as possible about their future child, that they should be given free choice which child to have, and "advice as to which child will be expected to enter life with the best opportunity of having the best life" (p. 425). Admittedly, making decisions which are in the best interests of others is, of course, a moral good. However, people have a greater moral responsibility to act according to the good of society as a whole. Humans exist and thrive within a social network, and if that social network is harmed, we are all, in turn, harmed. This means that moral decisions need to be made primarily at the social level for the good of all and this technology has been shown to lead to certain types of social instability.

The current use of sex selection technology is the prime example of the link between pre/post-pregnancy technology and social instability. The use of this technology in countries where there is a "combination of son preference, easy access to sex-selection technologies and abortion" (Hesketh & Jiang, 2012, p. 3) has led to unbalanced sex ratio at birth (SRB) rates. For example, in 2011, the SRB for China was reported to be 118 (National Bureau of Statistics of China, as cited in Hesketh & Jiang, 2012) – 118 males for every 100 females. Extensive use of ultrasound screening and selective abortion has led to approximately 30 million more males under the age of 20 than females (Zhu, Li & Hesketh, 2009). In India, one large-scale study reported that the SRB was 132 for second births when the first birth was a female and 139 for third births with two previous female births (Jha, Kumar, Vasa et al., 2006). While these skewed SRBs are also a result of better health care and food for boys, female infanticide and a high rate of death in childbirth (Allhbadia, 2002), it is clear from research that the use of sex selection technologies plays a significant role in the high male-to-female ratios (Jha, Kumar, Vasa et al., 2006; Zhu, Li & Hesketh, 2009).

The result of these unbalanced SRBs is that a significant proportion of men are unable to marry and this also leads to social instability.

Counter-argument for stance

Rebuttal

1st argument to support stance

Counter-argument

Rebuttal

2nd argument to support stance

In the countries mentioned above, social status is strongly related to marital status. Men who are left unmarried are largely the poor and uneducated, further increasing social inequalities (Lichter, Anderson & Hayward, 1995). High SRBs have been linked to increases in prostitution, kidnapping and trafficking of women in China (Tucker, Henderson, Wang et al., 2005) and in other parts of Asia (Hudson & Den Boer, 2004). Hudson and Den Boer also attribute a recent large increase in dowry prices in parts of India to the shortage of women. All of the above can lead to social instability. <u>While Savulescu might argue</u> that the parents of these male children have ensured the "best life" for their child, <u>this is not always true</u> as many of these males are likely to suffer from low self-esteem if they can't fulfil societal expectations such as marriage and procreation. One recent study using in-depth interviews, for example, showed that older unmarried men in Guizhou province reported feeling depressed and hopeless because of their single status (Zhou, Wang, Li & Hesketh, 2011).

It is also important to look to the future and consider the ethical implications of developing pre/post-pregnancy technology. It is feasible that technology might develop in the future to allow screening for desirable attributes related to appearance. **Ideals of beauty are social and cultural concepts. It has been shown that people who don't meet those ideals suffer discrimination.** For example, Judge and Cable (2004) found from an analysis of 45 studies that height was significantly correlated with career success and that a person who is 72 inches tall is likely to earn $166,000 more over a career than someone who is 65 inches tall. Widespread discrimination has also been shown based on weight in multiple domains such as the workplace, education and health care (Puhl & Brownell, 2001). <u>It might seem logical</u>, therefore, that parents use such technology to ensure the "best life" for their children. <u>In fact</u>, if we look at the effect on society as a whole, as we did with sex selection, it seems that a widespread use of this technology would lead to even less tolerance for diversity than exists now and therefore greater social inequality for those without access to such technology for economic reasons. This would lead to greater discrimination. What this means is that while there might be benefits for individual children born from the use of this technology, on the societal level, the effect would be much greater social inequality.

<u>Establishing an equitable and stable society is the responsibility of every individual who makes up that society. Establishing a society like this will sometimes require people to act against their own individual best interest for the sake of the greater good. The use of pre/post-</u>

- ← Counter-argument
- ← Rebuttal
- → 3rd argument to support thesis
- ← Counter-argument
- ← Rebuttal
- ← Summary of stance

pregnancy technology is an example of this. <u>While selecting traits such as gender and appearance might lead to individuals having a "best life", the harm that this does to society as a whole outweighs the benefits to the individual.</u> There needs to be regular and timely consultation about this issue between policy makers, ethicists, medical and legal professionals, and the general public.

Task 8
Identify language used to signal the counter-argument and the rebuttal

The table below shows language used to signal the counter-argument and rebuttal. These are only suggested answers; other answers are also possible.

Language used to signal the counter-argument	Language used to signal the rebuttal
Admittedly, . . .	Nevertheless, . . .
Opponents/critics of this potion believe that . . .	This claim is not justified because . . .
While is true that . . .	In fact, . . .
It might seem that . . .	This is not true because . . .
Some other examples	**Some other examples**
There is some truth in the fact that . . .	One objection to this is . . .
While . . .	This is not really the case because . . .
An argument against this is . . .	There are shortcomings to this claim because . . .

Task 9
Practise writing counter-arguments and rebuttals

Below are two example answers. Other answers are possible.

Issue 2: Nuclear energy should be the primary form of energy used by governments *because of its capacity to generate a large amount of power* [citation] ***needed by modern developed economies*** [citation]. *Admittedly, the set up costs are high* [citation] *and effect of an accident can be devastating* [citation]. *However, there are no alternatives, apart from coal, which can provide the amount of power needed around the world* [citation]. *A reliance on coal would* *have a far greater negative impact on the environment [citation] and in turn people's health, than the use of nuclear energy, even with a few accidents that are likely to occur.*

Issue 3: Factory farming (raising livestock such as chickens in confined spaces) should be banned *because this model of farming causes numerous health problems for the animals. For example, diseases can spread rapidly through the crowded population [citation]. This means the animals need to be fed antibiotics [citation]. When this meat is eaten, we in turn ingest these chemicals and this has been shown to contribute to a rise in antibiotic-resistant diseases [citation]. While it is true that this model of farming produces cheaper meat which could be used to increase the protein intake of the poor [citation], in fact, this kind of meat is largely being sold to fast food corporations to increase their profits [citation] which in turn has a negative effect on health.*

Remember:

You need to ask yourself the following question to decide when you need a citation:

Is this information general knowledge?

If **yes**, then it doesn't need a citation.

If **no**, then you would need to find a citation to support your stance.

Task 11
List hedging words

The table below shows some common examples of hedging words.

Frequency	Certainty	Quantity	
all the time	definitely	all	**Strong**
the majority of the time	certainly	numerous	
frequently	probably	most	
mainly	might	many	
often	may	in general	
sometimes	maybe	a bit	
rarely	perhaps	some	
infrequently	possibly	a small proportion	**weak**

Task 12
Improve a paragraph

An example of improvements can be seen on page 169.

~~I think it is really cruel to use live animals in experimental testing. It~~ **The use of live animals in experimental testing** should be allowed because of the benefits it brings to human health. This kind of testing has led to ~~amazing~~ **significant** improvements in medical treatments for cancer (Hausen et al. 2002) and HIV (Rickman et al. 2009). It has led to the development of **many/numerous** vaccines (Morgan et al. 2000) and medical treatments such as insulin (Nagano et al. 2005). It has also allowed scientists to determine the safe level of exposure to **a lot of/a large number of** common chemicals (Vanderberg 2010). Some opponents claim that these benefits are **commonly/frequently** outweighed by the suffering which animals endure and that other types of testing should be used instead, such as the use of cell cultures. This technique should be used when possible, however, its use is limited. Tests using cell cultures shows effects on the molecular level (Burns 2005) whereas animal testing can show systematic effects around the body. Legislative regulations have been put in place in **many/the majority of** countries to stop animals being ~~tortured~~ **harmed** in experimental research (Baumans 2004). These regulations are largely based on the three "Rs" first described by Russell and Burch (1959) – Replacement, Reduction, Refinement. For example, 1. animal tests should be replaced by other techniques, when possible, 2. the number of animal used should be reduced when possible and 3. experimental techniques used should be refined to ~~stop the agony and misery that the poor animals feel~~ **minimize animal suffering**.

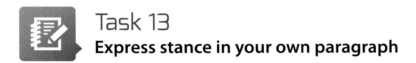

Task 13
Express stance in your own paragraph

An example of a paragraph can be seen below.

Euthanasia should be legal for terminally ill patients because it alleviates mental and physical suffering. Natan et al. (2010) found that terminally ill patients **typically** suffer from a significant amount of pain and depression. Although it is true that good palliative care **can** reduce mental and physical suffering **to a certain extent**, beds in good palliative care hospices are limited (Zerzan et al., 2000) because of inadequate government funding in **most** countries. Widespread research into palliative care has shown that that the **majority** of hospices give inadequate pain relief and inadequate counselling (Jennings et al., 2011). If a patient wishes to end their suffering, then doctors should abide by the ethical principle (Herring, 2012) to act in the best interests of the patient.

Clear stance with justification

Counter-argument

Rebuttal

Hedging (shown in bold and underlined)

ACADEMIC SPEAKING

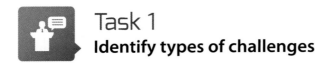

Task 1
Identify types of challenges

The table below shows the type of challenges.

Challenging the stance	What type of challenge could you use?
"People want GM food labelled."	Stance is overgeneralized.
"GM crops cause cancer. Rates of cancer have risen at the same time as the number of GM crops has risen."	Stance contains a cause/effect relationship which is wrong.
"All GM crops are unsafe."	*Stance is wrong.*
"We have to have GM crops, otherwise poor people will starve."	Stance appeals to emotion rather than logic.

Challenging the source	What type of challenge could you use?
"GM crops are more profitable for farmers. Even though GM seeds cost more, the overall cost from seed purchase to harvest is lower than conventional crops. An article from the *Journal of Trends in Plant Science* stated that GM seeds are, on average, 20% more expensive."	Ideas/statistics in source don't support the stance.
"Risk analysis shows that the benefits of GM crops far outweigh the negatives. This is confirmed by a 1996 study from the *Journal of Nature Biotechnology* which analyzed the case studies of 20 different GM crops."	Source is too old.
"Too much agricultural land is made up of GM crops. The percentage in the US is 16.5%."	*Evidence for stance is given but source is missing.*
"GM crops have the same environmental impact as non-GM crops. For example, a report by Monsanto shows that Roundup Ready corn has no worse impact than conventional corn."	Source is biased (Monsanto).

Task 2
Identify polite challenges

The table below shows some suggested answers. Other answers are also possible.

Challenging the stance	Example of challenging statement	Example of challenging question
"People want GM food labelled."	I **don't think** that is true for all people.	Are you sure all people want this?
"GM crops cause cancer. Rates of cancer have risen at the same time as the number of GM crops has risen."	I **wonder if** the rise in cancer is caused by something other than GM crops.	Could there be another reason for the rise in cancer other than GM crops?
"All GM crops are unsafe."	I **don't think** that this is possible. If it were true, a large percentage of the population would be sick.	Are you sure that is right?
"We have to have GM crops, otherwise poor people will starve."	That **might** be true but do you have evidence?	Do you have evidence for that?

Unit 4

ACADEMIC WRITING

Task 3
Read for stance

1. The writer's stance in this report is the following: While economic issues persist, the severity of the issues surrounding the environment in China requires immediate action and prioritization over the economic issues.

Task 4
Identify the writer's logic and argumentation

The box below shows the suggested answers for this task.

Stance
While there are economic problems, shifting focus to the environment is more important.

Supporting argument #1	**Supporting argument #2**
Government policies are insufficient.	Environmental problems negatively affect the economy.

Evidence given	**Evidence given**
1. Over 100 environmental laws, but ignored	1. Pollution negatively affects tourism and GDP
2. Beijing's poor air quality and visibility	2. Cost of pollution: USD100 billion or 5.8% of GDP per year
3. Tax policy unfavourable to renewable energy	

Refinement of stance in light of evidence
1. Regulations are important, but more is necessary.
2. Helping the environment can also help the economy.

Task 5
Identify the appropriate report section heading

4. Reasons for Shifting Focus to the Environment

The section heading "Reasons for Shifting Focus to the Environment" would be the most accurate because the section talks about placing more emphasis on the environment than the economy. However, the section heading "Environment" would not be accurate because it does not state the stance of the section.

Task 6
Write report section headings and identify topic sentences

Topic sentences are highlighted.

The topic sentence in section 2.1 accurately summarizes and states the stance of paragraph/section 2.1. This can be seen through the words indicating stance such as "decelerating" and "complications".

The topic sentence in section 2.2 accurately summarizes and states the stance of paragraph/section 2.2. This can be seen through the words indicating stance such as "issues" and "faces". This topic sentence also shows transition from the previous paragraph by using a linking phrase ("In addition") and repetition ("stagnant economy") for cohesion between paragraphs. The repetitive "stagnant economy" refers back to the main idea of the previous paragraph.

The topic sentence in section 3.1 accurately summarizes and states the stance of paragraph/section 3.1. This can be seen through the indication of stance in the clause "they are <u>partially alleviated</u> when <u>China's historical economic improvements are considered</u>". This topic sentence also shows transition from the previous paragraph by using a linking word ("While") and repetition ("the current economic risks mentioned in section 2.1") for cohesion between paragraphs. The repetitive "the current economic risks mentioned in section 2.1" refers back to the main idea of the paragraph in section 2.1.

Exemplar headings are in bold and have been written and underlined. Other headings are also possible.

2. Economic and Environment Challenges

This section discusses the challenges that China faces in its economy and environment.

2.1. Economic Concerns

Decelerating growth in China's GDP presents economic complications for multiple stakeholders. While China has seen unparalleled economic expansion in the past 30 years, many suspect that such expansion will not continue (2) (3). For instance, China's GDP most recently expanded by 7.7%, which was a decline from the previous period and markedly slower than expected (4). This slowdown can have negative implications for connected economies such as Taiwan, South Korea, Brazil, Australia, and Germany as well as Africa, which counts China as its third largest trading partner (5). Apart from outside stakeholders, Chinese rural workers have already been negatively impacted by their country's weakening economy (6). They reported that these Chinese rural workers were more adversely affected by the decline in growth than any other social group due to higher unemployment. Possible consequences include further income inequality, social unrest, and additional strain on younger generations who often need jobs to carry the burden of providing for their parents.

2.2. Seriousness of Environmental Problems

In addition to a stagnant economy, China also faces ongoing environmental issues. Among these include air pollution — a noticeably extreme problem — as China, according to Liu and Diamond (7), "has 16 of the world's 20 cities with the worst air pollution" (p. 37). A critical concern is that this statistic is likely to worsen. Coal, a major contributor to air pollution, accounted for approximately 70% of China's energy sources (8). Even with conservative assumptions in economic growth, Shealy and Dorian (8) estimated that China would still utilize over 6 billion tons of coal in 2025, which is three times that produced and used in 2005. Indicators measuring broader environmental factors also point to a deteriorating environment. Emerson et al. (9) report that China's environmental performance index in 2012 ranked 116 out of 132 countries analyzed and is trending downwards. In aggregate, these statistics show a debilitating environmental situation.

3. Shifting Focus to Environmental Issues

In light of the above overview on economic and environmental issues confronting China, this section provides justification for shifting attention from the economy to the environment.

3.1. A Strengthened Economy

While the current economic risks mentioned in section 2.1 are concerning, they are partially alleviated when China's historical economic improvements are considered. For instance, China's rapid GDP growth of 10% over the past 30 years has boosted its economy to the second largest globally (10). Apart from significant GDP growth as an indicator of improvement, the World Bank (10) reports that between 1981 and 2008, 600 million people were lifted out of poverty, representing a 71% decrease in poverty. A closer examination also reveals a more sophisticated economy. An example of this is China's shift towards a service-based economy, which has helped to raise wages and household income (11). This can potentially ease some of the high unemployment worries also discussed in section 2.1. Lastly, a declining Chinese economy is unlikely to be detrimental as current conservative predictions of 6.6% in GDP growth would still leave China on target to be a high-income country and to surpass the US in economic size by 2030 (12). All this suggests that the current economic challenges mentioned in section 2.1, after accounting for the improvements made to a weak Chinese economy 30 years ago, are manageable and perhaps less of a concern.

Task 8
Identify cohesion within a section

Section 3.2

In view of the relatively mild challenges on the economic front, a greater focus on the environment can be further justified in two ways. First, despite the severity of the situation, as discussed in section 2.2, existing policies designed to preserve the environment still show considerable deficiencies. Liu and Diamond (7) contend that "although more than 100 environmental laws and regulations exist in China, they are often ignored by local government leaders" (p. 37). A highly publicized example of the probable consequences of such weak enforcement is evident in the reporting of Beijing's poor air quality and visibility (14) (15) (16). Additionally, tax policies towards renewable energy projects have not been favourable; when compared with conventional energy projects, renewable energy projects often receive similar or higher taxation (13). However, the negative impacts of ignoring the environment are apparent not only in the environment, but also the Chinese economy. Statistics on tourism and GDP, two economic indicators, show that pollution in China has had damaging consequences (17) (18). The extent of the economic damage from worsening environmental conditions has also been measured. The World Bank (19) calculated that the total cost of outdoor air pollution and water pollution to China's economy was approximately USD100 billion or 5.8% of GDP per year. Assessing the above, it is clearer that government policies and regulations for the environment require immediate attention. Perhaps even more significant, the aforementioned evidence strongly suggests that a greater focus on the environment rather than the economy would help to improve both.

Task 9
Categorize and identify cohesive devices and strategies

Referencing	Lexical repetition	Linking words and phrases
<ul><li>two ways – first</li><li>environmental laws and regulations – they</li><li>such – ignored by local government leaders</li><li>the above – (refers to arguments presented in this section/ paragraph)</li><li>the aforementioned evidence – (refers to evidence presented in this section/paragraph)</li><li>both – economy – environment</li></ul>	<ul><li>environment – environmental conditions – environmental – pollution – worsening environmental conditions</li><li>economic – economy – taxation – GDP</li><li>policies – environmental laws and regulations – government policies and regulations</li><li>such weak enforcement – they are often ignored by local government leaders</li><li>damaging – economic damage</li><li>measured – calculated</li><li>environment – renewable energy – conventional energy</li><li>consequences – negative impacts</li><li>both – environment – economy</li></ul>	<ul><li>however</li><li>also</li><li>more significant</li><li>example</li><li>additionally</li></ul>

Task 10
Understand the reasons for synthesizing

Below is the explanation for synthesizing and the relationship between the sources.

The writer wants to use multiple sources to enhance the credibility of the information being cited. The relationship between the sources is that the sources are reporting similar information.

Task 11
Synthesize overlapping and contradictory information

These are only suggested answers; other answers are also possible.

(1) One possible synthesis:

Not only have companies not prioritized environmental issues, they have strongly resisted the notion of considering environmental issues (Smith, 2010; Ellis, 2011).

(2) One possible synthesis:

Reallocating resources from the economy to help the environment will not be popular since jobs will be lost (Tompkins, 2010). However, a lack of concern for an environmental issue such as air pollution will increase nitrous and sulphur dioxide, which are both harmful pollutants (Lin, 2009).

(3) One possible synthesis:

While reports from Chu (2010) and Chan (2009) showed that sulphur dioxide levels had increased, the more recent economic slowdown has caused levels of sulphur dioxide since 2010 in Southern China to fall by 5% (Lu, 2013).

Task 13
Write a cohesive and logical paragraph

These are only suggested answers; other answers are also possible.

Justification for Improving the Environment ◄— — — — — — — — — — — — → Heading shows stance and is written as a noun phrase.

While economic concerns persist, a renewed focus on the environment rather than on the economy can positively impact both. Concerns about the economy arise from statistics that show a significant slowdown in the Chinese economy, with the most recent indicators showing just an 8% growth rate, which represents a 40-year low (Lan, 2013). When viewed from a domestic perspective, this provides justification for further supporting the economy rather than the environment. However, a global view of China's economic growth shows that an 8% growth rate is higher than most developing nations (Smith, 2013). Additionally, a closer examination reveals several relationships between the economy and the environment. According to Fung (2010), the Department of Environmental Protection attributed $6.5 billion USD worth of economic damage to water and air pollution. This is likely due to powerless government policies and regulations. To lower air pollution, many laws have been enacted to reduce coal consumption in multiple areas of China (Xu, 2011), but they are often "ignored or given very little importance in many parts of China" (Li, 2012, p. 25). By prioritizing the environment over the economy, the government could better ensure the enforcement of regulations and prevent similar economic losses in the future. **Another way of recouping these losses is by providing economic incentives for entrepreneurs to open businesses and employ workers with the objective of reducing water and air pollution (Fung, 2010), which would also help to reduce worries of social instability from high levels of unemployment (Xiao, 2013).** An existing successful example of this solution is in the US, where such businesses profited over $10 billion USD and hired more than 300,000 people since 2001 (Fung, 2010). Therefore, placing more importance on the environment than on the economy could be beneficial to both.

Topic sentence shows stance and summarizes the paragraph

Words in purple are examples of lexical repetition for cohesion

Words in blue are examples of linking words for cohesion

Words in red are examples of referencing for cohesion

• Example of synthesis of two sources within a sentence

ACADEMIC SPEAKING

 ## Task 1
Link appropriately to what others have said

Below is the explanation to why Transcript C shows better linking.

Transcript C shows better linking with the content of Transcript A. Transcript C uses agreement language "Yeah, I think what you're saying about the worsening conditions in Southeast Asia is true" to show a link to what was said in Transcript A. Additionally, Transcript C presents a different perspective by mentioning that the economy is also important, but links this perspective with Transcript A's discussion of worsening environmental conditions in the last sentence. Transcript C not only uses agreement language to link, but also makes its content relevant.

Transcript B, however, only uses agreement language. It is not known whether the student who said Transcript B was listening to or understood the student who said Transcript A. This is shown by the sudden shift in perspective to Southeast Asian economies without any mention of or reference to the environmental issues mentioned in Transcript A. Transcript B uses agreement language, but does not make its content relevant.

Task 2
Prepare notes for a short discussion

The table below shows the answers to the categorization of notes in this task.

Information that supports the stance of helping the environment	Information that supports the stance of helping the economy
Relates to economic impact	**Relates to economic impact**
1. 2012 – Water and air pollution cost economy $6.5 billion USD	1. Economy weakened considerably in 2012
2. 2012 – Economy still growing at a steady pace of 7%, which is higher than most developed countries	2. 43% care more about economy than environment – still large percentage
3. Financial incentives can be given to entrepreneurs to open businesses to clean and prevent pollution	3. 2012 – employment slowed to 8% growth – slowest growth in jobs in 40 years
4. Pollution clean-up companies in US made $10 billion in profit and created 300,000 jobs	
Relates to legal issues	**Relates to legal issues**
1. Laws aimed at limiting use of coal – often gone ignored in many parts of China	1. Many regulations already exist to decrease use of coal in various parts of China
Relates to health issues	**Relates to health issues**
1. Air pollution has devastating effects on health, e.g. asthma and lung cancer	1. Many health cases – patients had pre-existing health problems – may not be due to air pollution
2. Cardiovascular (heart) problems from air pollution	
Relates to social instability	**Relates to social instability**
1. Air pollution → angry citizens → social instability	1. Taking resources away from economy → fewer jobs → unhappy citizens → social instability

Unit 5

ACADEMIC WRITING

Task 2
Identify the stance

This table summarizes the *stances* and *main arguments* in the essay and report.

Essay	Report
Overall stance: Critical of RTV – it does more harm than good.	**Overall stance:** Critical of RTV – inappropriate content for children.
Main arguments: 1. RTV is immoral – humiliating and deceptive. 2. RTV endangers contestants – there should be better legislation.	**Main arguments:** 1. Children have difficulty understanding and responding appropriately to RTV "reality". 2. Children watch too much RTV unmonitored by parents, particularly using new digital media.

The two texts have a similar stance as they are both **critical of reality TV**,

however, whilst the essay focuses on **issues of the genre to a general public**,

the report focuses on **why it might be damaging for children.**

Task 3
Identify broad structure

There are many different features students might notice in this task. See Task 4 below for a summary of these features.

Task 4
Summarize structural similarities and differences

This table summarizes the main similarities and differences in structure between the academic essay and report.

Similarities in structure	Differences in structure
1. Both texts begin with an **introduction** and end with a **conclusion**	1. The report has headings, **subheadings** and a **numbering** system to facilitate comprehension. The essay uses **topic** sentences for this purpose.
2. Both texts contain a clear **stance** with two main **arguments**	2. After presenting the two main arguments, the report has a section covering **solutions**, whilst the essay has a paragraph of **counter-arguments** .
3. Both texts contain **counter-arguments** and **rebuttals** to balance the main arguments.	3. The report has an additional section after the introduction giving **background information** . This kind of information is presented in the essay's **introduction** .

Think again . . .

Academic reports and essays are generally expected to include:

✓ An introduction, conclusion and main body paragraphs/sections.

✓ A clear stance, counter-arguments and rebuttals.

✓ Both academic reports and essays will include some form of background information at the start. (See the point below.)

Extra comments relating to the table:

· The number of arguments/counter-arguments varies in both texts depending on the complexity and length.

· Depending on the topic, reports often, but not always, contain a recommendations or solutions section.

· Reports may have an additional background information section at the start, including for instance, terminology, statistics, or facts. If less background is needed, this will probably be included in the introduction, as in the essay.

Task 5
Identify the functions of introductions and conclusions

This table compares the main functions of the introduction and conclusion in the essay and report you have analyzed.

Academic essay: Introduction	Academic report: Introduction
• **Opening statement** (introduces essay focus) • **Background statistics** (popularity of RTV) • **Statement of stance** (RTV could be educational, but the need to entertain is more powerful) • **Outline of essay** (including shape of essay – stance then C/A; repeated stance)	• **Background information** (compares past/now) • **Report focus** (issue of uncontrolled access to inappropriate shows) • **Statement of stance** (children's RTV viewing is a concern) • **Outline of report** (background statistics, two concerns and solutions)
Academic essay: Conclusion	**Academic report: Conclusion**
• **Stance restated** (extended with imagery to add weight to argument) • **Future prediction** (open questions about possible future scenarios – these also act as a **summary of key issues**)	• **Stance restated and summary of key issues and solutions** • **Recommendation** (further empirical research is needed)

Both introductions in this unit include: **background information, reference to the essay's/report's focus, a statement of the stance and an outline.**

Both conclusions in this unit include: **a restatement of stance and summary of key issues.**

Task 6
Create links backwards and forwards between sections

Topic and final sentences

Links are created between sections and paragraphs as follows:

Topic sentences:

1. The first part of the sentence (**before** the comma) refers to: **an idea from the *previous* paragraph or section.**

2. The second part of the sentence (**after** the comma) refers to: **the main idea *in its own* paragraph or section.**

Final sentences:

Both final sentences look forwards to **the main idea in the *next* section** as follows:

- The next section (Section 2) describes the *negative impacts* on children.

- The next section (Section 3) describes *solutions that include regulation and education*.

Reference to data and sources

The following table shows three ways in which data and studies are referred to in the two texts. There are a few more examples in the report; these are shown on the complete text analyses above.

Type of reference	Example	Location
a. Backwards reference to statistics	*(see above), Some of the above figures.*	report, section 2.1
b. Backwards reference to a study	*the Girl Scout Research Institute survey (see above) indicates that the same girls . . .*	essay, paragraph 4
c. Forwards reference to a diagram	*See Figure 1 below . . .*	report, section 1

Task 7
Write a group report

This is one example of a possible plan for this task, written using short note forms. You might like to compare it with your own if you need further ideas before you write.

Plan: Report on Teenagers' Use of Technology

Introduction

- General statement about worrying increase in use of technology among teens today
- Background info: statistics/facts. Games and SNSs most prevalent.
- Stance: teens vulnerable to content bullying on SNSs + it negatively impacts mental/ physical health
- Outline: first 2 main issues, then solutions to them

1. Negative impacts of teenagers' technology use
Two issues: 1. SNSs and cyberbullying   2. Computer games and risk to mental/physical health

1.1 Risk of cyberbullying
SMSs public – incr. in online bullying & inappropriate content
Reason: X using privacy setting & parents X monitoring
E.g.: Online bullying survey – alarming
C/A: Southern Europe better, e.g. Spain has +ve reports on impact of sites.
R: Same Spanish article (above) argues for education to stop posting of neg. comments

1.2 Risk to health from computer games
Teenagers too much time playing computer games; too little time outside → physical + cognitive problems
Physical problems examples + Cognitive problems examples   (statistics/facts)
C/A: Examples of positive health impacts
R: Negs outweigh positive, hard to deny teens less active/unhealthier today

2. Measures to address the problem
Ways to address two issues mentioned above. Increase choice of activities: govt, schools and parents.

2.1 Tackling the issue of cyberbullying
Responsibility three places: SNSs themselves, schools and parents.
E.g.: Measures from each
Potential results/implications

2.2 Reducing health risks from gaming
Balance must be found – get teens outside and moving more.
Poss thro gvt schemes, examples
Potential results/implications

Conclusion

- Restate stance + summary of key points
- Recommendation – govt & schools need to take this seriously, if not prediction: problems may escalate.

Essay: Analysis of features of structure

ESSAY	Features of Structure
The recent phenomenon of reality TV, although hugely popular worldwide, has at the same time met with considerable audience disapproval (Poniewozik et al., 2003). Its influence can be seen in outstanding ratings, for instance the 2012 final of *Britain's Got Talent* attracted an audience of nearly 14.5 million (*"Britain's Got Talent"*, 2012) and the Nielsen Poll of Top US Prime Time Television 2012 placed seven reality shows in its top twenty.[1] Whilst such impressive audience figures indicate that reality TV could function as a valuable educational medium and promoter of civic values, this is not the priority of most money-making broadcasting networks whose main aim is to entertain. This essay will first discuss various moral issues of the genre, then move to consider how educational and social benefits generally come second to the demands of cheap entertainment, sometimes at the cost of individuals.	**Introduction** **Statement of main focus** + expert quote **Background** statistics **Stance:** Brief mention of benefits (C/A) followed by main stance = critical of RTV **Outline** of essay = Arg → C/A → rebuttal
The main argument against reality TV is a moral one. Reality shows are often described as "humiliating" ("Is Reality TV Too Cruel?" 2012) and "deceptive" (Papacharissi & Mendelson, 2007). The weaknesses and misfortunes of participants are revealed as audiences enjoy a display of hopefuls who can't sing, cooks who can't cook, and other failures. As Poniewozik (2003) indicates, what is remarkable about this "discomfort TV" is the ability of participants to rise above their insufficiencies. But this is the thing that Poniewozik believes audiences find so appealing; the message appears to be that in the pursuit of dreams, embarrassment can and will occur, but we actually have the power to rise above failure and live to fight another day relatively unharmed. Whilst the humiliation of candidates who choose to appear on a game show where the "rules" are known is quite possibly acceptable, it becomes questionable when contestants are openly deceived, as in *Joe Millionaire*, where women compete for the favours of a construction worker pretending to be a millionaire.	**Stance 1** Topic sentence with **stance 1** (*RTV = immoral*) Development of **stance** (*humiliating and deceptive*) **Evidence** from Poniewozik + writer's interpretation **C/A:** (*acceptable on these grounds*) **Rebuttal:** (*but not acceptable when there is open deception*)
Humiliation and deception are definitely a concern, but more worrying is the effort some shows go to in search of new and often dangerous ways to maintain audience ratings. In some extreme competitions, participants take part in dangerous challenges for which they are ill-prepared, such as extreme rock climbing or rafting, and accidents do happen. A *Survivor* participant was recently admitted to hospital with serious burns and a	**Stance 2** Topic Sentence – looks **back** to previous paragraph and **forwards** (to **stance** of this para. = (*dangers of RTV*)

Wipeout participant suffered a stroke ("Is Reality TV Too Cruel?" 2012). Other shows depict people in dangerous situations, committing crimes such as drunken driving or underage drinking and it would seem to be unclear as to what kind of legal obligation, if any, producers might be under to protect the individual. This is a point echoed by Wyatt (2009) who emphasizes that contestants are largely unprotected by basic workers' rights. Indeed, working conditions may be intentionally worsened to provoke extreme reactions, the key to successful reality TV. Much needed legislation has been introduced successfully in some countries, but if pushed too far, this might be interpreted as state interference in public entertainment. A case in question is the recent decision by China to limit the number of reality TV shows to two a week per network ("China to limit", 2011). More could still be done to protect individuals against possible dangers.

Despite the questionable ethics of reality TV, there are some critics who consider it to have social and educational merits. Poniewozik (2013), for example, favours watching competition shows with his family. He claims that by viewing the world through others' eyes and experiences you gain unexpected new insights. For instance, following a business startup show, he realized "what a fascinating process conceiving and valuing a business is" (p. 54). Nevertheless, his principal motivation for watching would still appear to be a good evening's entertainment, not to receive an educational experience. Ouellette (2010) recognizes that reality TV is melodramatic, but still argues for its civic value in promoting self-empowerment, inspiration for volunteerism and charity in shows, such as *Extreme Makeover* and the *Secret Millionaire*. This point is supported by a recent survey from the American Girl Scout Research Institute of girls aged 11 to 17, where 75% agreed that "the shows depicted people with different backgrounds and beliefs", and 62% that "they raised their awareness of social issues and causes".[2] This could also help address discrimination, encourage tolerance and normalize co-operation between social groups that are divided by gender, race, ethnicity and sexual orientation. Some argue though that these shows could still do more to challenge stereotypical representations (Sears and Godderis, 2011; Bell-Jordan, 2008) and racial division (Rothman, 2012). Ultimately, any possibility for social and educational benefit should be weighed carefully against the findings from studies revealing negative influences. For instance, the Girl Scout Research Institute survey (see above) indicates that the same girls who claimed to be inspired by reality shows seemed also to have gained an inaccurate understanding of social norms and acceptable behaviour from their viewing.

Examples and **evidence** (incidents, expert opinion, legal situation + student's **interpretation**, e.g. *it would seem to be unclear…*

C/A: *(legislation is being passed)*

Rebuttal: *(legislation can be seen as "interfering").*

Counter-argument
Topic Sentence – looks **back** first, then **forwards** to the **stance = C/A** (social & educ. merits).

1 *(educational value-* Poniewozik) + **rebuttal** *(entertainment more important).*

2 *(civic value –* Ouellette) + **rebuttal** *(staged, melodramatic)*

3 *(awareness of social issues)* + **rebuttal** *(incorrect understanding of social norms –* see end of paragraph).

4 *(challenge stereotypes)* + **rebuttal** *(they don't go far enough).*

Final **rebuttal**: Overall, despite some positives, negatives are firmly evident.

Undeniably, reality TV has over the last ten years become a popular expression of contemporary global culture, one which certainly could help bring about learning and good citizenship. However, in order to satisfy ratings and turn profits, these shows are heavily driven by the need to entertain rather than the need to educate or encourage social values and this, in turn, can impact audiences and participants negatively. Very few people switch on a reality show wanting to learn how to cook the perfect pavlova or to start a business on £150; rather, we watch to enjoy the public humiliation of an amateur cook with a collapsed soufflé or the dramatic boardroom shaming of an over-confident business hopeful. Like the Roman amphitheatre, reality TV is predominantly satisfying popular demand for uncomplicated sensation and entertainment with less concern for morals, ethics or taste. Its future depends on whether it continues to seek the largest possible audience, whether states apply censorship to control its excesses, or whether its potential merits are exploited to promote social harmony.

Conclusion
Restatement of issue and **main stance**.

Main arguments restated with vivid examples from RTV (shared reality).

Future predictions based on arguments made in the essay. It closes with open questions that relate to three main issues discussed.

Report: Analysis of features of structure

REPORT	Features of Structure

Introduction

Not long ago, children were raised on a diet of *Sesame Street*, *Disney* and *Scooby Doo*, with the occasional sitcom and wildlife programme. Parents were secure in the knowledge that their youngsters were exposed to nothing unsuitable, and might possibly learn something too. Today, the situation has radically changed. Reality TV (RTV) has replaced the old sitcom at the top of the TV ratings (Nielsen, 2011), appealing to broadcasting networks with its popular and cheap-to-produce content. Digital access to hundreds of channels on demand makes these shows more accessible, whilst presenting new challenges for parents. This report maintains that the amount of RTV children are watching is a serious concern, particularly in light of the growing number of online multimedia viewing options. It begins by examining recent statistics relating to children's RTV viewing, then moves to consider two particular areas of concern. Finally, it considers ways broadcasting networks, governments and parents might best address these issues.

Introduction

Background information: comparison of past and present with names of popular shows to create interest.

Evidence of popularity of RTV, therefore **significance** of topic.

Intro. to **main focus of** report: digital access creates challenges for parents.

Main stance: concern over children's viewing of RTV.

Outline of report structure: background info, two areas of concern, solutions.

1. Children's viewing habits

Various polls indicate that children, young and old, are watching a worrying amount of television, in particular RTV, most of which was originally designed for adults. According to the UK-based Broadcaster's Audience Research Board, BARB (2011), most of youngsters' viewing occurs noticeably *outside* traditional children's airtime, peaking between 20:00–20:30, and this is true of both older and younger children. It is no surprise then that reality TV constitutes a large proportion of the TV diet for children of all ages. In fact the same BARB report states that it actually accounts for five out of six of 10 to 15-year-old children's favourite shows in the UK (see Figure 1 below). These statistics lead both experts and parents to question its potential impact on children.

(Figure 1: . . .)

Figure 1: Top 6 TV shows, 2011, all children aged 10–15. Source: BARB, 2011.
(Reality shows are shaded green.)

2. Potential issues in children's viewing of reality TV

The issues surrounding children's viewing of RTV are complex. This report focuses on two key areas: the difficulties children have connecting the reality they see on TV with the reality in their own lives, and the unlimited, unmonitored access to RTV afforded by new media.

2.1 Inability to distinguish between reality and fantasy

Research suggests that younger children, especially those under eight, are less able to differentiate between reality and fantasy than their elders (UMHS, 2013). As a result, they may accept the graphic images, violent language and contrived scenarios of RTV as reflections of "real" life, causing nightmares and leading them to imitate aggressive behaviour (AAP, 2001). Teenagers too are often unaware of the degree to which reality is manipulated. In a recent survey of girls aged 11–17 from the Girl Scout Research Institute (2011), 75% believed that competition shows and 50% that real-life shows are "mainly real and unscripted". This demonstrates a failure to understand the degree to which reality TV is edited and constructed. Furthermore, the girls' agreement with certain statements (see Figure 2) implies they both expect and are more tolerant of what might

---

Section 1: Background

Topic sentence stance: *Children are watching too much RTV*

Supporting evidence 1. + implications

Supporting evidence 2. + implications

Forward reference to table: *"See Figure 1 below"*

Final sentence: points forward to section 2.

Notice the information given below the Figure relating to the diagram. This is first referenced in-text above.

Section 2: Issues of RTV

Short lead-in to section, introduces two main issues/stances: *"difficulties w. RTV reality & unlimited, unmonitored access"*

Stance 1

The subheading indicates stance: *children have difficulties differentiating reality from fantasy*

Evidence 1. + interpretation

Evidence 2. + interpretation

Evidence 3. + interpretation

be termed "negative characteristics" than girls who do not watch RTV regularly.

> "Gossiping is a normal part of a relationship between girls" (78% vs. 54%)
>
> "It's hard for me to trust other girls" (63% vs. 50%)
>
> "You have to lie to get what you want" (37% vs. 24%)
>
> [% watching show vs. % not watching show]

Figure 2: "Varying perceptions of girls who watched and didn't watch RTV." Source: Girl Scout Research Institute (2011).

Although the same girls (see above) could recognize that many shows set a negative example, and some of the above figures might look relatively low, this does still indicate that a significant proportion of youngsters have unhealthy views as a consequence of watching RTV.

2.2 Unlimited access to inappropriate shows

It is not just what youngsters watch but also how they watch and for how long that concerns many parents. Rideout et al. (2010) state that two-thirds of US children have televisions in their bedrooms for unsupervised viewing. Whilst this is worrying, even more disturbing is the recent US statistic that 8 to 18-year-olds' combined average media use (cell phones, iPods, laptops, etc.) increased from 6.21 hours a day in 2004, to 7.38 in 2009 and that the largest part of this is spent watching TV, which is actually equivalent to an adult's full working week (Kaiser Foundation, 2010).

It is unlikely that many parents know exactly what their children are watching unmonitored on these new platforms, although considering youngsters' RTV preference (see Figure 1), one might presume they are watching similar shows, as well as more inappropriate RTV originating from later time slots. This is why finding ways to regulate RTV content and educate children about its shortcomings must be a priority.

Forward reference to table: *"See Figure 2"*.

Counter-arguments

C/A 1. *although all of the girls recognized . . .* & **C/A 2.** *some figures might look low* + **Rebuttal:** *this does still indicate . . .*

Backward reference: ("see above"), *"Some of the above figures"*.

Stance 2

Subheading indicates stance

Topic sentence looks **backwards** (*what*) and then **forwards** (*how and how long*).

Evidence 1. + interpretation

Evidence 2. + interpretation

Extended interpretation of situation.

Backward ref. to section :1 *"See Figure 1"*:

Final sentence restates stance, its significance & points forward to section 3.

3. Addressing the issues

This section will consider a range of ways to address two issues: confusion of reality and fantasy and unlimited access to inappropriate shows.

3.1 Helping children distinguish between reality and fantasy

By watching RTV together as a family, parents can make an important contribution, engaging their children in critical conversation that helps them recognize how "reality" is constructed in these shows and is therefore essentially "unreal". This would encourage "active viewers" rather than a "passive audience" (Holmes, 2004). Talking about the real-life consequences of immoral behaviour and comparing television reality with their own reality can help children apply what they have seen to their own lives in a healthier way. Schools might also play a role, teaching children to analyze content, for instance, by debating moral issues from the shows in Media Studies classes. Professional organizations such as the Parents' Television Council (2012) and The University of Michigan Health System (2013) provide useful web-based resources to support parents and schools in encouraging children to engage in this way.

3.2 Tackling the issue of unlimited access to inappropriate shows

This is a complicated issue with a range of responses, from direct censorship, to various parental measures.

3.2.1 Governments and broadcasting networks: Tighter regulations

External monitoring and legislation are two extreme ways of ensuring appropriate content, especially when children are most likely to be watching. Some networks have disputed the regulatory approach, as did Fox TV unsuccessfully in 2012 (Flint and Savage, 2012). In China, the State Administration of Radio, Film and Television has limited satellite channels to two reality programmes a week ("China to limit", 2011), and in India, two shows with "vulgar language" and "objectionable scenes" were moved to a later slot (Burke, 2010). Although such censorship is problematic in a free society and it also does not completely solve the problem of unlimited access on mobile devices, in passing tighter regulations, governments are, nevertheless, communicating a vital message to broadcasting networks to be more careful about content.

3.2.2 Parental measures: Internet filters, setting time limits and educating by example

Whilst legislation can have its uses, it is almost certainly parents who have the greatest potential to bring about change. It is highly advisable they are familiar with the latest RTV programme content to exercise informed control over their children's viewing. One way of doing this is by studying networks' own ratings. The US television industry, for instance, has a ratings system which can be linked to a V-chip, allowing parents to block unsuitable programmes. In addition to this, anxious parents can utilize a wide range of parental control software (e.g. NetNanny, Netflix and Hulu) to block offending programmes, or alternatively, they can block access altogether to the TV and Internet at certain times of the day.

Solution 3: Also addresses problem 2.2

Option 2: Topic sentence looks back to 3.2.1 then introduces 3rd solution = parental control.

The above measures all relate to parental controls, it is essential, however, that parents also take a proactive role in setting a good example. For instance, given that parental programme choices are known to strongly influence those of their children (Parents Television Council, 2012), they should select their own viewing carefully. Similarly, they should limit their viewing and switch off unsuitable RTV shows, whilst explaining why they are doing so. Further positive habits could be fostered by encouraging children to participate in healthier activities such as sports, drama and music, and engaging in these as a family sometimes too.

Topic sentence looks **back** first "*The above measures*", then introduces second parental angle "be proactive".

Conclusion

Reality TV has established itself in global culture, and children everywhere will continue to be exposed to it in the foreseeable future. The problems many children have responding appropriately to adult-oriented content are very real, and aggravated further by today's pervasive Internet access. Various control mechanisms and efforts to improve critical awareness are needed. Parents are key to both, but schools, governments and broadcasting networks may have a part to play as well. Beyond this, more empirical research on the impact of the media on children's development would be useful in identifying content to be avoided.

Conclusion Restatement of **situation, stance** and **summary of key issues** and **solutions**.

Recommendation: In addition to measures mentioned above, there should be more research.